# then SHE said IT

*a play*

## Osonye Tess Onwueme

African Heritage Press
San Francisco   Lagos
2002

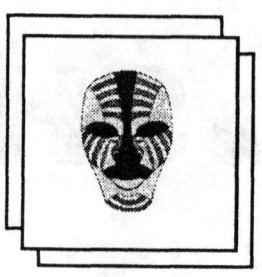

## African Heritage Press

P.O. Box 170613  
San Francisco  
CA 94117  
Phone: 415-469-8676  
e-mail: afroheritage9760@aol.com  
www.africanheritagepress.com

**Lagos**  
23 Unity Road  
Ikeja,  
Lagos, Nigeria  
Phone: 234-080-331-28151  
       234-4972044  
e-mail: infoplan2000@yahoo.com

---

Copyright © 2002 Osonye Tess Onwueme  
ALL RIGHTS RESERVED  
No part of this play may be represented, reproduced, performed or copied without the formal permission of the author.

---

Cover Design: Kou Thao

ISBN 0-9628864-2-4

Library of Congress Catalog No. 2002101216

Onwueme, Osonye Tess

www.tessos.com

[Selections 2002]

*then* **SHE** *said* **IT**

-Theatre, Drama, Africana Studies, Cultural Studies, Women Studies, Political Science, Postcolonial Studies, and World Literature.

for you
my mothers
whose elastic strength and grace
even in life's crossfires
bind me
to rise again
 and again
always
when I fall
as I do--

maria ndidi (mama lagos)
cledie taylor (mama detroit)
ifenyinwa osamor (mama ifi-ogwashi)
adankwo nwa ogada (mama ubulu)--

And
for you
nonso
a son so beloved
how dare you depart
so hastily
into the eternal void
that taunts and roasts
me...us now?
how dare you,
nonso?

# Other Creative Works by *Osonye Tess Onwueme*

*Shakara: Dance-Hall Queen.* San Francisco: African Heritage Press, 2000.
    Winner, the 2001 Association of Nigerian Authors (ANA) Drama Prize.

*Why The Elephant Has No Butt.* San Francisco: African Heritage Press, 2000.

*Tell It To Women.* Detroit: Wayne State University Press, 1997.
    Winner, the 1995 Association of Nigerian Authors (ANA) Drama Prize.

*Riot In Heaven.* San Francicso: African Heritage Press, 1997.

*The Missing Face.* San Francisco: African Heritage Press, 1996.

*Three Plays.* Detroit: Wayne State University Press, 1993.

*Legacies.* Ibadan: Heinemann Nigeria Ltd., 1989.

*The Reign of Wazobia.* Ibadan. Heinemann Nigeria Ltd., 1988.

*Mirror for Campus.* Ibadan: Heinemann Nigeria Ltd., 1987.

*Ban Empty Barn & Other Plays.* Ibadan: Heinemann Nigeria Ltd., 1986.

*The Desert Encroaches.* Ibadan: Heinemann Nigeria Ltd., 1995.
    Winner, the 1985 Association of Nigerian Authors (ANA) Drama Prize.

*The Broken Calabash.* Ibadan: Heinemann Nigeria Ltd. 1984.

*A Hen Too Soon.* Owerri: Heins Nigeria Publishers, 1983

# ABOUT THE AUTHOR

Born in Nigeria, Osonye Tess Onwueme has established her reputation as the leading African female playwright with national and international distinctions in Africa, Europe and North America. She attained both her B.A and M.A degrees from the University of Ife, and her Ph.D in Literature from the University of Benin, Nigeria. Her outstanding achievements include: substantial grant awards for her writing and stage production from the Ford Foundation in 2000 and 2001, three times winner of the Association of Nigerian Authors (ANA ) Drama Prize for her plays; *Shakara: Dance-Hall Queen* (2001), *Tell It To Women* (1995), and *The Desert Encroaches* (1985).

From April 27-May 28, 2001, her highly acclaimed play, *The Missing Face*, had its international premiere, off-Broadway, at the Woodie King Jr.'s New Federal Theatre in New York City.

Furthermore, she has won the following prestigious awards for her writing: the 1988 Distinguished Authors Award, the 1989/90 Martin Luther King/Ceaser Chavez Distinguished Writers Award, the 1993 Nigerian Eagles Award, the 1994 Nigerian Achievement Award in Literature, as well as the 1995 University of Wisconsin System's Award for Excellent contributions by the Women of Color. Her published works include: *A Hen Too Soon* (1983), *The Broken Calabash* (1984), *A Scent of Onions* (1986), *Ban Empty Barn And Other Plays* (1986), *The Artist's Homecoming* (1986), *Mirror for Campus* (1987), *The Reign of Wazobia* (1988), *Parables for a Season* (1990), *Some Day Soon* (1991), and *Riot in Heaven* (1996). In 1994, she joined the University of Wisconsin, Eau Calire, Wisconsin, as the institution's first Distinguished Professor of Cultural Diversity, & Professor of English. Among the institutions she has taught are: Vassar College, Poughkeepsie, New York, Montclair State University, Montclair, New Jersey, Wayne State University, Detroit, MI., the University of Ife, Nigeria, Federal University of Technology, Owerri, Nigeria, and Imo State University, Okigwe, Nigeria.

# Production History of the Drama

Following the 2000-2001 generous financial support of the Ford Foundation, the play was first staged at the State Cultural Centre, Calabar, Cross-River State Nigeria, on July 6, 2001, with actors and crew members from the Nigerian Theatre Guild. Though the play was subsequently adopted for Command Performances by the Delta State Government, and was directed by David Orere, the following were the original cast and crew, who toured the major cities of the Niger-Delta states with the production:

## The Cast

| | |
|---|---|
| OSHUNA | Mina Joda |
| ATLANTIC | Bassey Ekpo Bassey |
| ETHIOPE | Sunday Umana |
| NIGER | Affiong Okon |
| BENUE | Eme Ekanem Enyamba |
| OBIDA | Ekakem Ekpenyong |
| KOKO | Nsa Honesty |
| KAINJI | Thomas Etuk |
| OJI | Norman Do Noor |

## Drummers/Activists

| | |
|---|---|
| Ufford Ikike | Raymond Inyang |
| Archibong E. Asibong | Morris Bassey |
| Victor Thompson | Ita Okon |

## The Technical Crew

| | |
|---|---|
| Artistic Director | Chris Nwamuo |
| Lighting &Sceneography | Molinta Enendu |
| Choreography: | Raymond Inyang |
| Costumes | Margaret Akpan |
| Make-Up | Ann Okon |
| Publicity | Itoro-Obing Etuk |
| Stage Manager | Jide Ogunkilede |
| Sound | Pius Kumengisa |
| Property Master | Hilary Elemi |

# SYNOPSIS

No longer able to contain the seething pain of silence and indignity, her voice finally erupted and broke through the guarded prison walls, where she had been subjected to exist (or die many times!), since her life-time. Then she said it! At last, 'Mama Said it', amplifying the many choking voices of her wounded daughters in the ravaged land of Hungeria, typified in the drama. Echoes of the women's tortured voices shock and slash through the entire body of the nation, and beyond, as the people cry out loud: How long can a people, whose land produces the richest oil and natural gas resources for the controlling local national and foreign interests continue to suffer and exist in, Silence? Abject Poverty? Hunger? Starvation? Acute Fuel, Water and Electricity Shortages? Violent Rape and Abuse of Women and Girls? State Terrorism and Genocide? Displacement? Environmental Pollution? Massive Corruption? Humiliation and Betrayal, especially in the hands of those elected and entrusted to protect them? In the drama, these nagging questions and concerns fuel the struggles of the rising militant and radicalized women and youths of the metaphoric state of Hungeria (as Nigeria?) to speak out and 'drum' them in this dramatized revolutionary struggle for change and challenge to tradition. Determined to never again be silenced and intimidated by their oppressors, the relegated women now take centre-stage to 'stage' their pain, and project their cause to the international community, who can no longer ignore them, as they are compelled to grant them a hearing for justice. Their main target, however, is to confront and destabilize the multinational forces and class interests that have, for long, impeded and humiliated them all, individually and collectively.

These multinational forces/interests are typified in the play by ATLANTIC (the foreign oil director), KAINJI, and the national Government Official, with the Traditional Chief, ETHIOPE, ironically, charged and entrusted to protect the people's lives and interests. Betrayed and dispossessed, the wounded people resort to militant action and protest. They march forward to press their demands for their just compensation, human rights, dignity, and the freedom to control the resources of their own land. This turbulent movement for change in the drama is driven by the joint forces of the radicalized Youths, together with the hurting Market Women and Mothers of the land.
OSHUN, who was a prostitute and mistress of the foreign oil director, until he blatantly snubbed and insulted her, now leads the Activist Youth Movement, with her girlfriend, OBIDA – who, in spite of her high educational achievements, has suffered the indignities of unemployment, rape, and violent abuse from her uncle, the Traditional Chief that 'sold' her for profit to the overseas oil merchant from whom she later escaped without her uncle's knowledge.

Reinforced by the activist leaders of the Market Women, NIGER and BENUE, whose husbands and sons were already slaughtered in the violent struggle against the conniving powerful forces, the activists bribe the local policeman, guarding the exclusive (in)famous iron gates of the GRA Oil Club, in order to gain access to invade and kidnap the privileged members of the GRA Oil Club. Then tensions rise and escalate beyond government control. The protesters set ablaze the oil pipelines and refineries, until the GENERAL, the elected national president of Hungeria, declares a State of Emergency and orders his security forces to shoot at sight any suspected activists, and erase their entire village. This irrational order by the government further adds gasoline to the fire. Tension, and violence engulfs the entire nation, leading to the arbitrary arrest of the activists, including the old market women, NIGER and BENUE. The growing saga peaks in the Epilogue: A Nation In Custody, where the imprisoned old widows and youths are tried and prosecuted before an imagined World Jury. As a resolution, this International Jury returns a NOT GUILTY verdict for the People of Hungeria Against the State. Furthermore, the Jury rules against the oppressive transnational forces of the government and its allies, demanding that the convicted powers not only pay adequate compensation, but respect the rights and dignity of the people of Hungeria, in addition to the conscious institutionalization of a genuine North-South Dialogue between the contending parties and interests.

## THE SETTING

*All actions take place in the fictional State of Hungeria. There are two main activity areas. One is marked the GRA/OIL CLUB, with the sign: RESTRICTED AREA. KEEP OFF! A locked iron gate shields this restricted area, with all its nuances of affluence and upper-class habitation. Opposite this area is the bare surrounding of the Market-Square, which is the main frontier of the community's life activity and struggle. There are no solid structures to inhibit the flow of the people's movement. Only the barricaded empty fuel station stands out in this open market-place.*

# CHARACTERS IN THE PLAY

*Please note that all the fictional characters in this play are named after rivers or bodies of water, both big and small. While the smaller waters act as youths, evolving and changing roles, the bigger ones remain fairly constant, even in their dynamic change of course. Note, too, that when the actors are not engaged in specific roles, they join the rest of the restless crowd. Though some individual characters might play significantly important or dominant roles, the drama is not specifically about them. But rather, like the swift currents of water that defy limiting boundaries, these promethean characters both embody and project the dynamic change or movement that transforms the life and consciousness of a people, hanging on the cliff of existence and power.*

---

OBIDA: The 23 year-old school niece of the Traditional Chief is an unemployed school teacher, who grows into a militant force in the people's movement.

NIGER: A 45 year-old widow, and leader of the market women. With her unemployed restless children and militant youths, she takes strides in leading her people's struggle for change.

BENUE: With her friend Niger, and the militant youths, the 43 year-old widow and mother lead the market women and the people's struggle.

OSHUN: The 21 year-old rebellious daughter of Niger and mistress of the foreign Oil Director (Atlantic). Though well educated, she's unemployed. Rebuffed by her white master, she grows into the beacon of her people's revolutionary struggle for change.

KOKO: The 19 year-old unemployed daughter of Niger and younger sister of Oshun. A good friend of Obida, she plays the role of Hawker/Seller, and a leading role in the struggle.

KAINJI: A 21 year-old unemployed son of Benue. He plays the role of Government Official, Oshun's lover, Guard, Police, General and Fuel Attendant in the drama.

ETHIOPE: A 23 year-old unemployed youth, who plays both the role of Businessman and Traditional Chief closely allied with the Government Official and the foreign oil director.

ATLANTIC: The 27 year-old powerful foreign oil director, and a close ally of both the Government Official and the Chief. Oshun is his mistress.

OJI: In addition to other roles in the drama, this 20 year old unemployed youth also plays the role of Prosecutor, Oshun's Lover, and Priest/Friend of Atlantic.

# PROLOGUE

*The action begins now at the center of the village market-square. The space looks bare, tired and sleepy, except for the glowing crescent moon, hanging in one corner of the dominant blue-gray sky. At first, a strident drumbeat greets the world, but it is soon silenced by the avalanche of gun-shots, explosive sounds, war-drums, and angry voices, descending on this tired land. A sudden shrieking sound follows as two limping, terrified young women flee from their locations in the audience to center-stage. Wounded and out of breath, they support, nurse and comfort each other until they break into a spiritual/blues song. But that too is disrupted when two frightened youths (male and female), running from some invisible assailants, come crashing on them with their shouts: "They're coming again! Help! Save us! They'll kill us! Help! Help! Save us!" The girls try their best to help until the number of refugees swell beyond their power to control with the wounded, especially, the older women, gathering there to seek refuge. All around, they continue to comfort and nurse the traumatized who still cry out loud: "They took her...tore her up right before me. See! See what they're doing to me at my age!" an old woman cries out. "You too, mother? Aaaah!" Then another: "They killed him...shot him point-blank right before me!" "Just like they did to my husband and son!" another replies.*

*Suddenly, siren-sounds cut into their tired voices as heavily armed men storm the scene from all directions, forcing this wounded community into a more alarming, urgent race for life and survival. They try to run in different directions but a youth is captured and held hostage as the others escape. For a while, thick shrouds of silence drape the land, until one by one, they start to re-emerge, angry, defiant, determined to be no longer crippled with fear or silence. With everyone gathering, soothing and holding on to the other, they slowly form a human chain until they break into songs of solidarity. The first fugitive youths have become so animated by their experience, they lead the people's song, and provoke them into dialogue with the audience. The drama has begun.)*

YOUNG WOMAN: You see? It's how it's been with us. See? Now tell me, how long can anyone continue like this?
CHORUS: How long? How long?
YOUNG WOMAN: Don't you think it's time? Time to take our case to the people... In short, the world?
CHORUS: Yes, the world! People of the world. Let them judge. Give the ver-

dict! Yes, hear us! Hear us and judge for yourselves!
YOUNG WOMAN: So you're ready to tell them then?
CHORUS (*Warming up.*): Oh yes! We are. Ready!
YOUNG WOMAN: Are you sure? Remember they can arrest you for speaking out? Jail you for life without trial. Charge you with arson. Murder. Are you ready for more persecution?
TWO VOICES (*Frightened.*): Oh no...Not again. They'll kill...
ANOTHER YOUNG WOMAN (*Fiercely*): Yes, let them. We're down on the ground already. So what else can they do?
YOUNG MALE & FEMALE: True. What else can they do to us?
CHORUS: What else-what else-what else?
YOUNG WOMAN: So you're ready to tell your story then?
CHORUS (*Resounding.*) Yes!
YOUNG WOMAN: You are?
CHORUS: Yes!
YOUNG WOMAN: Ok, then. You take your destiny into your own hands. It's your choice. So now, go ahead and tell the world your...what you're going through.
CHORUS (*Chanting.*) Yes, about time. Our story! Hear! Hear! Hear us!
WOMAN: Now women, beat, beat the drums!
YOUNG WOMAN: What did Mama say?
CHORUS (*Pounding their feet.*): Beat! Beat! Beat the drums! (*Drumbeats rise.*) Beat! Beat! Beat the drums!
YOUNG WOMAN: What Mama said-What Mama said...
CHORUS (*Breaking into dance.*) Women, beat, beat the drums!
YOUNG WOMAN: And so she said it!
CHORUS: Women, beat! Beat! Beat the drums! (*Unified, they break into vibrant dance-steps. Meanwhile, the Young Woman quickly exits behind and returns with a box-full of clothing, house-hold items and whatever else is required to dramatize their experience. The people are so animated as they distribute the items and they dress up for their new roles. Thus transformed, some begin to mime and adjust to their new characters, while others set up the stage. Once the stage is set, they quickly form a human chain, pounding the earth with their feet. Suddenly a loud explosion shatters their world. Chaos, as the people scream and flee into all directions. Blackout. The drama has entered another stage.*)

# MOVEMENT ONE

*(Right side of the market-square. It's a hot afternoon in the GRA/Oil Club. Seated, and playing the game of Monopoly around a lounge-table with a canopy above it are the powerful allies: ATLANTIC as the foreign director of the oil club, KAINJI as the national Government Official of oil, and ETHIOPE as the traditional Chief. A large TV screen mounted above broadcasts the day's news reports. An empty chair, a stool with a speakerphone-set and a radio on the other with drinking glasses, mark ATLANTIC's space from his partners. The men remain absorbed in their game, until the TV anchorman directly presents the angry protesting mob: "We can't wait! We won't wait! Enough is Enough! We can't wait! We won't wait!" This irritates ATLANTIC, and he quickly switches off the radio, cursing under his breath: "Damn! These people! There we go again?" He lights a cigarette, presses the speakerphone and calls out: "More Service!" OSHUN, quickly steps out from inside. Her red short skirt, sleeveless blouse, which taunt the eyes, rudely announce her agile, youthful body mounted above platform shoes. Like a seasoned waitress, she bears a tray of alcoholic drinks and glasses. She greets the men, bends down to serve them, with their greedy eyes poking into her as they're caught in marking the geography of her body. ATLANTIC is most affected; he quickly loses interest in the game, pulls her into his bosom, and sends his hands to work and wander around her willing body. Meanwhile, his equally distracted partners try to sustain the game.)*

KAINJI: Man, that's some deep, deep waters you're in. Mind you get drowned.
    *(They chuckle, each one pushes his own game forward.)*
ETHIOPE: Yes. Easy. Take care, my friend.
ATLANTIC *(To OSHUN.)*: Sweetie. More, baby. More! *(Lifts his glass, toasts.)*
OSHUN: To you. I'm at your service.
ATLANTIC: My express service from Venus! Not so?
SHUN *(Smiling seductively.)*: One thing you got right!
ATLANTIC: Yeah. My special brew from Hungeria! Let's drink to that.
    *(He toasts, this ime with the men. The Chief obeys but appears uncomfortable with the apparent vulgarity.)*
ATLANTIC *(Still fondling.)* You belong to me, Babe.
OSHUN: Now.

ATLANTIC: Sure? (*Yawns, runs fingers through hair.*) So unruly. Babe, I need...
OSHUN (*Leaving.*): A shave.
ATLANTIC: You got it.
OSHUN (*Still Smiling.*) Positive. Play on. I'll soon be back. (*She picks up the empty glass, steps back seductively into the door. Her sister, KOKO, appears as the Seller/Hawker with OJI, now approaching as a jobless man. She's carrying a fruit basket on her head, while the joblessman is armed with his machete. At the gate they break into a call-response chant:* "Buy my Pawpaw! Sweet like Sugar! Buy my Pawpaw!" *Then the unemployed man throws up his machete, flips and turns it into a javeline as he chants:* "I Sabi cut grass! Try me! I fit cut grass! And fertilizer? I fit put am too! Just try me! Oga try me!" *When he stops, the Seller/Hawker takes over. ATLANTIC simply gives them a spiteful look and curses under his breath:* "These lazy bastards!" *In response, the Government Official says,* "Can't trust any of them. Just a bunch of nuisance. Let's play, my friend." *That said, the men resume their game. Tired of being ignored, the solicitors leave.*)
ATLANTIC (*To the Chief and Government Official.*): Should I trust her?
ETHIOPE: Who?
ATLANTIC: The girl.
KAINJI: OSHUN? But why not?
ATLANTIC: You know...these people...Well, I don't know. We'll see.
ETHIOPE: Hnm...I'll tell you what the monkey said about trust. 'I tell you I can trust the baby that I'm still carrying in my womb. The one behind my back, well, how can I tell?'
ATLANTIC: Interesting. So...?
ETHIOPE: Don't misunderstand me. I know her...I mean, her mother, leader of the market women.
ATLANTIC: I guess you do. You *know* every woman in the entire region. (*Laughter.*)
ETHIOPE: I try. (*Silence.*) Believe me, nobody from the other side or tribe will dare to come... I mean cross the line.
KAINJI: True. The boundary is marked with fire. Can't you hear them? (*They listen. Angry voices of the community, screaming:* "Commot! Go! Go back to your land. No! You can't continue to take the jobs when, we're here. Go! They already gave you people the local government headquarters. What else do you want? To take everything? Ok, here? Come and drink all the oil with your oyibo! You dogs of the white man!")

ATLANTIC: You hear that? Everyday, war. Agitation. The pipelines are no longer safe. We're losing money...Losing staff...Drilling oil here is fast becoming a dangerous business. (*Pause.*) Hnm...OSHUN. I wonder why she's taking so long. What is she up to now?

KAINJI: Taking her time to make up. You know them...

ETHIOPE: Women? Hazardous...Ha!

ATLANTIC (*Rising.*): Let's see... (*He disappears behind the closed door. The Chief and the Government Official are now alone.*)

ETHIOPE: You know he's right.

KAINJI: Yes. But we're also doing our best.

ETHIOPE: And our best's not good enough?

KAINJI: Maybe. But then, where do we go from here?

ETHIOPE: Just last week, the Deputy Director of hell...

KAINJI: You mean Shay...?

ETHIOPE: Oh, well...you know what I mean? The Shame Vice...

ATLANTIC (*Returning.*): Yes, poor Jack! You know my deputy narrowly escaped from those hooligans?

ETHIOPE: So we heard.

ATLANTIC (*Sighs.*) Who knows what they're going to do next?

KAINJI: And now they're poaching in the oil pipelines just because of their greed and...

ATLANTIC (*Drinks.*): Set the damn thing ablaze!

KAINJI: In the Jesse-Delta explosion, two thousand and fifty people dead!

ATLANTIC: See?

ETHIOPE: Mostly women and children.

ATLANTIC: Life is cheap in Africa. Ha!

KAINJI: Unprecedented mass suicide.

ETHIOPE: Genocide.

KAINJI: And who's to blame but the people themselves?

ETHIOPE: Blame the victims?

KAINJI: Well, who is...?

ETHIOPE: Isn't.

KAINJI: But who cares, anyway? The oil pipelines are clearly marked '**Restricted Area. Out of Bounds to all unauthorized persons.**' But no. They're blind. Deaf. What were they doing there, anyway?

ATLANTIC: Praying! Chanting, 'Jesus Saves!'" Ha! Ha! Ha! You tribes-people are a trip! Africa! Just look around you. Seen Rwanda? Somalia? Liberia! Sierra Leone? And now here, Hungeria? (*Chuckles.*) Well, now I understand the true spirit of the Organization of African Unity. Quite a great specimen of ritualized Organized Assassins' Union. The

OAU. Ha! Ha! Ha! For a people so outstandingly endowed with...with passion, you know. That special brand of progress? Made in Africa, huh? Just one thing I know my Africans are doing right, at least. *(Mock laughter.)* Gentlemen, it's worth celebrating. Celebrate. Let's celebrate the organized animals' united genocide! It's the great tradition of being Born-Again-African...bloodbath. Drink! Drink to it! Africa's success stories. *(Toasting.)* To Africa's united planned progress in genocide! Ha! Ha! Ha!
*(His partners stare at each other. Silence.)*
ATLANTIC: Why look so morose? Is it not true? Friends, I'm proposing a well deserved toast to your people. Let's drink.
ETHIOPE *(Pushing his game.)* Play. *(Reluctantly, they respond to the toast.)*
ATLANTIC: Yes. Let's keep on playing. *( Back to the game.)*
KAINJI: Will they ever learn?
ETHIOPE: Who?
ATLANTIC: *Your* people.
KAINJI: Black...
ATLANTIC: It's in the blood...in the blood...*(Sighs, stretches.)* Scary, isn't it? Well, we need security reinforcement. I've sent for more.
ETHIOPE: For whom?
ATLANTIC: My people, of course!
ETHIOPE: I hear you.
ATLANTIC: We need more security guards.
ETHIOPE: But you have so many guards already.
ATLANTIC: One can't be too safe.
ETHIOPE: Our people don't joke with their land. To them, Land *is* Life.
KAINJI: Perhaps, one can't blame them. What is a man worth without land, anyway?
ATLANTIC: Stocks! *(Mock laughter.)*
KAINJI: Not for these people. They'll kill anyone they think's an enemy.
ATLANTIC: I know now why my British predecessors called this, "the city of blood".
KAINJI *(Interrupting.)*: But they too killed millions.
ETHIOPE: Took millions...
ATLANTIC *(Laughing.)*: And the summary again? Life is cheap in Africa! *(He breaks into mock laughter as he pushes his own game forward.)* But I know how to deal with anyone who crosses my line. *(Turning to OSHUN who has just walked in with his shaving kit.)* Hear that, my sweet Papaya? *(She nods her approval, goes behind him, and teases him with the blade as if beheading him.)*

OSHUN: You asked for it. Are you now ready to be shaved?
ATLANTIC (*Runs his fingers through his hair.*) Unruly stuff. Huh? I just can't wait.
OSHUN: Ready then? (*She starts to sharpen the blade. (ATLANTIC turns to examine the blade.)*
ATLANTIC: Not sharp enough yet?
OSHUN: I've told you... Just wait and see. (*She starts to sharpen the blade as ATLANTIC observes the shaver with obvious discomfort. He checks the blade again.*)
ATLANTIC: Too sharp! You're butcher or what?
ETHIOPE: Want to kill the man?
OSHUN (*Loud Laughter.*): Won't be the first. (*Calmly to ATLANTIC.*) You're afraid?
ATLANTIC: Of course not! But that blade you have looks too sharp. Scares the shit out of me...any man... (*To the men.*) Gentlemen, please check this.
ETHIOPE (*Inspecting the blade.*): Seems right to me, my friend.
ATLANTIC: True?
KAINJI: You bet your life on it.
ATLANTIC (*Laughing.*): Yours too. Life's too precious, my friend.
ETHIOPE: For all of us.
KAINJI: Absolutely!
ATLANTIC (*Looks at his watch.*): Let's hear the news. (*ATLANTIC presses the remote control. The screen shows the mob, protesting and chanting anti-government slogans in a non-violent demonstration in the streets. In silence, the men watch the action, while OSHUN, who seems absorbed in the chants, sings along with the mob: Ozugo-o! Ozugo! Hell. Hell. Shame go-go! Hell-Shame go go-o! Mob-Mobil. Mobilize-Mob! Mobilize Mob! Commot. Hell. Shame go-goooooo!*
ATLANTIC (*Pulling her onto his lap.*): Babe, tell me. What are they saying?
OSHUN: Listen. I'll show you. (*Swinging her hips provocatively.*)
ATLANTIC (*Teasing.*) Bad girl! Can't depend on you. No use. (*Meanwhile, the people's drumbeats intensify as OSHUN turns up the volume and entertains them with her modern dance-movements. Amused, ATLANTIC mutters "Rascal! Such a rascal!" Then he turns away from her to the men.*) My friend, tell me, what the hell are they singing?
ETHIOPE/CHIEF: Shame!
ATLANTIC: What?
ETHIOPE: That Shame must go.

ATLANTIC: Nonsense! These idle people! Won't they go find some job?
ETHIOPE (*Pushing his own game.*): Where?
KAINJI (*Playing.*): Haven't we tried enough?
ATLANTIC: Precisely! We've tried everything to help them.
ETHIOPE: They're not satisfied.
ATLANTIC: Until they begin to drink with our skulls?
ETHIOPE: Well, they just want more. (*Nudging ATLANTIC to play, but his eyes are now glued to OSHUN who's still absorbed in her dance.*)
ATLANTIC (*Realizing himself.*): Ah. Are *your* people ever satisfied?
KAINJI: Depends.
ATLANTIC (*Still distracted.*): On whom?
ETHIOPE (*Pushing his own game.*): You...Your turn, Director! (*But ATLANTIC's lost in thought.*)
KAINJI (*Nudging ATLANTIC harder.*): We're waiting. Play!
ATLANTIC: Oh, can't you see? Keeps me busy... (*OSHUN stops dancing, falls into ATLANTIC's arms.*)
ETHIOPE: And forgetful?
KAINJI (*Laughing.*): Messed up?
ATLANTIC (*Applauding her.*): Great, girl! Sure know how to turn a man's head! (*She stands behind ATLANTIC and places the shaver on the nape of his neck. ATLANTIC jumps.*)
ATLANTIC: Ouch!
OSHUN (*Still laughing.*) Jumping from a common blade? Our master is a coward.
ATLANTIC: You blame me? I love my life.
OSHUN: Who doesn't?
ATLANTIC: Well...(*Changes his mind, pulls his head away.*) You know, girl. I don't really think I'm ready for this now.
OSHUN: Later then?
ATLANTIC: Yes. These gentlemen are here for business.
OSHUN (*Packing up her shaving kit.*) Good-bye then.
ATLANTIC: Are you leaving me?
OSHUN: Oh, no. Don't worry. As sure as death, I'll be back to take care of you! (*Chuckles.*)
ATLANTIC: That's my sweet... (*He's silenced with a kiss from her. OSHUN tunes into a reggae station on the radio, then starts to leave. She's consciously, provocatively swinging her backside with him lustfully staring at her.*)
ATLANTIC (*Shaking his head.*) A riot, that girl!
ETHIOPE & KAINJI: She is!

(OSHUN *steps aside with her loaded bag that she now clutches on to her chest. Their hawkish eyes trail her steady strides up to the gate until lights fade out on her and the visitors take their leave of* ATLANTIC. *The screen is still on.* ATLANTIC, *stands alone, watching the protesting mob, with their drumbeats:* "We want jobs! We want food! We want homes! Shame must go! Agep must go! Chefron must go! Texas must go! Agep must go! Mobile must go! Webros! Killbros-Webros must go! Pollution! Pollution must go! Leave! Leave our oil! Leave! Leave our land! Oil! Oil! We have the oil! We want our oil! Oil! Oil! Oil! We want our land! We want our Resource! Resource! Resource! Resource Control!" *For a moment, the protests continue. It's mixed with voices of the angry mob, shoving, quarreling among themselves, until one loud voice shouts* "Unite! Fight the enemy and not yourselves!" *This is followed with rowdy questions:* "Who? Who? Who's the enemy? Show me the enenmy! Show me the enemy!" *Someone points to the Oil Club:* "There! There!" *Suddenly, everyone else takes up the tune which soon grows into a choral chant of* "There! There! There is our enemy! There! There! There is the enemy! There is the enemy!" *The crowd gets more agitated, amplified by the chants into a marching tune. At first, their voices and chants are discordant, but as they begin to march and face the direction of the GRA/Oil Club, they find harmony and the tempo rises until they move, surge forward in angry uproar toward the exclusive villa.)*

# MOVEMENT TWO

*(Like many other villagers, hunting for food, water and other essential commodities, OSHUN and OBIDA have joined the crowd of waiting hustlers gathering to buy fuel and kerosene at the barred Fuel/Petrol station in the market-square. As the long waiting and chattering continues, OSHUN displays some of the toilet tissue, soap and other household items she's taken from the villa, and now shares them with her friend.)*

OSHUN *(Sharing the goods.)*: I'm back. See?
OBIDA: Trouble...
OSHUN: Call me 'Lucky.'
OBIDA: Ok, Lucky Trouble! *(They laugh.)*
OSHUN: I told you. I wasn't born to suffer. My mother says to me always; 'if you can't see how to do it, then do as you see it.'
OBIDA: Lucky, your mother's there to teach...You know my story. *(Tearfully.)* They killed...killed my father for this oil...And...and then, my mother? Gone. Gone!
OSHUN *(Cuddling)* I know. So painful your mother, too, became a victim of that oil pipeline blast.
OBIDA: Poor mother. Just died like that. And to know that she joined the oil poachers just minutes before that girl brought the lantern. And then the explosion. Mother had got nothing. Nothing. Not even a drop of fuel. But she was cooked... fried...fried in that sizzling... Aaaah... *(Sobs.)*
OSHUN: Don't cry, my dear. I feel your pain. We all do. But we can't change that now. What has happened has happened and we will now have to look to the future. It will never happen again. Never! We won't let them!
OBIDA: But my parents are gone.
OSHUN: Well...Not really. Your parents are resting in the arms of their creator. And they hear you...us now. *(Pause.)* You think they're sleeping? No! I believe they're all here...all our people slaughtered and butchered for asking to get a bite, just a slice of what belongs to them. No dear. Our dead do not sleep. Neither will our God. So cheer up. Have faith. Resource control. That's all we ask and yet they won't let us. They shoot and kill us.
OBIDA: So terrible! Took so many precious lives...*(Stops.)* And that greedy uncle who could have saved this whole community? Where was he?

Where?

OSHUN: Don't mind the yeye Chief. He thinks we don't know what he's doing with those thieves. We'll make them pay. All of them.

OBIDA: Careful, though. Those people are callous.

OSHUN: I know. (*Excitedly dangling a bunch of keys.*) Guess what? I got the key to..

OBIDA: To his heart!

OSHUN: Much like it. You know, I can enter anywhere in that villa.

OBIDA: He gave them to you?

OSHUN: How can? They're so shrewd, those people. Make you turn in every key to them as you leave everyday. My response? I made myself copies. They really think we're fools. (*Pause.*) Well, we'll keep playing the fool to get what we want. Ha! They'll see! Just who's fooling whom?

(*They chuckle.*)

OBIDA: The day they'll catch you? Hnm...They'll tear you open like they did those poor Odi-Choba women. They'll make you sweat.

OSHUN: In my anus. Ha! Ha! Ha!

OBIDA: Just that? They'll tear... rip you apart. Rape you right before your mother.

OSHUN: Then rape my mother too and force me to watch.

OBIDA: Ahaa! We all know. They think they'll always do what they like and get away?

OSHUN: No way! Never again. And that's why we must deal with them.

OBIDA (*Chuckling.*): By stealing their soap and toilet paper? Well, they have too much. They won't even notice.

OSHUN: Until they've been shaved clean. (*Pause.*) Have you seen KAINJI yet?

OBIDA (*Saluting.*) To lick him hot? Razor-girl! Ride on!

OSHUN (*Strutting.*): I'm Naija-Hot, you know? You think they call me that for nothing?

OBIDA: That I see. Go ahead. Shave all the men clean.

OSHUN: But not my KAINJI. I want him. (*Pause.*) Have you seen him?

OBIDA: No. That boy has so licked the fire into you that your bottom sweats, just to lose sight him for one minute.

OSHUN: Say what you like. I love him. I need him to travel with.

OBIDA: Your handbag? We know.

OSHUN: Any girl who takes a man as her handbag knows she'll go empty-handed.

OBIDA: And you're not.

OSHUN (*Gyrating.*): Girl, I need him. Want him so bad now. (*Turns to go.*)
OBIDA: But can't you wait for fuel?
OSHUN: I already gave the can to my mother. KAINJI's all I need now. (*Departing.*) I'll go check him up at his security post.
OBIDA: So he got the job?
OSHUN: Of course! What did you think?
OBIDA: That anyone, even the director can easily smell the love oozing from both...
OSHUN: Too bad for him. He can do anything, whatever. But he can't hide the sun. Can he?
OBIDA: No. Haven't I told you what they did to me? That man?
OSHUN (*Soothing her.*): Who?
OBIDA: That one who calls himself my uncle. (*Showing her masked face with scars.*) See what they've done?
OSHUN: I know. Greed.
OBIDA: Those white directors are even more terrible. They just have too much power and think they're clever.
OSHUN: Yes. Until they cross me. (*Pulling her.*) Come.
OBIDA: Tell me how you did it.
OSHUN: What? With KAINJI or ATLANTIC?
OBIDA: Well, both. You know...How come ATLANTIC hired him as his personal guard?
OSHUN (*Swings her hips provocatively.*): He thinks he'll take me for nothing? (*They laugh.*) He tells me that he loves me. That he'll do whatever he can to please me. So I set a trap for him. Pushed KAINJI on to him to give him a job. At first, he refused. Said he didn't like or trust the boy. That in any case, he'll need to consult first with the Government Official and the Chief.
OBIDA: Those crooks!
OSHUN: Well, I quietly stayed away for days.
OBIDA: Then he got itchy!
OSHUN: And hungry. No one needed to tell him where to find the food. He sent for me, asked to see my brother. And KAINJI got hired!
OBIDA (*Laughing.*) With you! Bad girl! Now I see how you both got the job! Spider! Spinning your webs all round! (*OSHUN does some gyrating, with OBIDA joining.*)
OSHUN: Do we have a choice? We've got to survive.
OBIDA: But how? See what they're doing to us. What are we going to do?
OSHUN: With these people?
OBIDA: Who else? Our lives depend on them.

OSHUN: No. You mean *their* lives depend on us?

OBIDA: Oh, well... If only they'll try to be honest and accept the truth for once.

OSHUN *(Seriously.)* Look, my friend. I've told you the best way for us to deal with this people is to do something. Something shocking. Terrible...

OBIDA: Like killing them?

OSHUN: Well, that too. But it's no use, killing.

OBIDA: There's too much of that already.

OSHUN: So what do we do?

OBIDA: We need...need...try something...something new *(Pause.)* Like kidnapping?

OSHUN *(Lighting up.)*: Yes! The Director, with the gang leaders of the oil club!

OBIDA *(Excitedly.)* Great! Wonderful! Always full of ideas! *(Hugs OBIDA.)* That's why you'll be my friend, always. Yes! We'll teach them a lesson.

OSHUN: Bring national...

OBIDA: And international attention to our cause!

OSHUN: That's it! That's when they'll start to pay attention to us and our needs.

OBIDA: Isn't it sad?

OSHUN: Well, if that's the only way they hear, we'll use any means to reach them.

OBIDA: And then the press...media?

OSHUN: Those too! They'll have a feast. Blow it to the roof top. Chant it night and day. *(Play-acting. "This is the Hungerian breaking news! Oil Director kidnapped by village women! Leaders of the oil club abducted by rural women and youths! Man-hunt is now underway to find them. And the kidnappers have named their ransom: Three Billion! We'll keep you informed about any developments!" The play-acting ends. The girls burst into laughter.)*

OSHUN: What a life where only the violent and tragic make news!

OBIDA: We'll share this with our people when we meet.

OSHUN: I must find KAINJI now. Absolutely important that he stays on our side.

OBIDA: Does he have any other choice?

OSHUN: Well, who knows with these men? *(They laugh. OSHUN starts leaving with the lights following her until they fade into the next stage.)*

## MOVEMENT THREE

(*The Marketplace. A bold sign at the fuel station: NO FUEL. OBIDA has joined the hustling and chattering of the mob behind the barricade leading to the fuel pump. They're pushing, shoving and cursing one another as everyone struggles to edge their way into the crowded space near the pump/hose. OBIDA pushes her way through the chaotic line, goes over, pumps and plays with the empty fuel hose. A male voice shouts: "Yes sistah. Pump am! Pump am well-well! I dey your side!" Then another male replies: "Girl, pump it! Pump it to me! Give it to me! I'm ready!" The tense air breaks lose, as the starving community now rocks with laughter.*)

OBIDA: Are they selling?
BENUE: Tomorrow.
OBIDA: Then why wait? What for?
BENUE: Tomorrow. Patience, my pickin.
OBIDA: Patience? I'm tired! So tired, Anti. How long must we have to wait?
NIGER: A good question! (*Laughter. They see the Fuel Attendant approaching with an armed Police and quickly resume their struggle for space in the line, with the cursing and pushing intensifying. Like generals inspecting an army, the Fuel Attendant, with the Police behind him, now struts in front of them to show-off the dry hose. He pumps out empty air, then blares out: "See? No fuel! No Kerosene! Go away!" But the people know better; they defy his order and trade more banter.*)
NIGER: You know when they do that?
BENUE: Means there's fuel.
OBIDA: Scare tactics, always.
NIGER: That's the spirit. They think they're clever? Can you catch an old hen with mere chaff?
BENUE (*Teasing.*): Old layers like you should know better! (*They laugh.*)
NIGER: And you? A spring chicken at 50, eh? Ha! What about those who can't do anything since they can't even find one short pump or limp hose? (*Laughter.*)
BENUE: Tell me about that!
OBIDA: Well, Anti, we plead guilty. Some of us. And those of us who got laid...
NIGER: Poor child! So you teachers have also joined the tribe of the unemployed, ehn?

OBIDA: Anti, na so we see-am-o!
NIGER: But why? So who takes all that oil money? And who'll teach the children?
BENUE: Vultures!
NIGER: Both local and foreign breed. (*General laughter.*)
BENUE: See? See them hovering in the land?
OBIDA: What do they care?
WOMEN: Yes, what do they care?
NIGER: Except for their own mouths and bellies. 'Dem-dem' only.
BENUE: And is that why they should lay off half the workers just because they say they want more profit and can't pay all that salary?
OBIDA: And did you hear how much the so-called leaders spent renovating their mansions in the state capital?
WOMEN: No. Tell us.
OBIDA: Billions!
WOMEN (*Alarmed.*): Ehn?
OBIDA: Enough to feed this nation for centuries!
NIGER: And here we are.
BENUE: Begging.
OBIDA: Just to be able to survive.
WOMEN: One day? Just one more day! (*Pause.*)
OBIDA: And look around you. See? They're not even killing us alone. The trees too!
NIGER: Our farmlands!
BENUE: And Rivers!
NIGER: The environment.
BENUE: Polluting.
NIGER: Polluting the land, the rivers, our entire environment...
WOMEN: All polluted.
OBIDA: You said it.
NIGER: Then she said it.
OBIDA: They've killed everything with their oil pollution and spillage. We cannot breathe clean air. Fishes die or get fried in the polluted simmering rivers. Water -water everywhere. But we have no clean water to drink! And now we lose the land too?
NIGER: No firewood because the plants and trees are soaked in oil. What do they expect us to cook with?
BENUE: Your arms and legs!
NIGER: Our men's runt sticks! (*Again the women break into laughter.*) My sisters. I'm not leaving here until I get what I need.
OBIDA: Yes, mothers. We must stand up for our...

OJI/ OLD MAN (*Joining them.*): Rights in this country. Yes. You're not alone, my sisers! Guess how long I've been waiting here? Since yesterday.
OBIDA (*Alarmed.*) You mean you had to sleep here?
OJI/OLD MAN: What else? No water. No food...
OBIDA: And sleep?
WOMEN: Tomorrow! (*They all laugh. They spot some shady movements behind.*)
OJI/OLD MAN: I smell something fi... fish...
OBIDA: Fuel! It's there. (*Pause.*) Always deceiving us. Send us away so they can sell at bloated prices to their friends loaded with...
NIGER (*Still laughing and moving forward.*): They're not fooling me. I'm going to wait here till I get what I want!
BENUE (*Pushes forward.*): Me too!
NIGER: These people think we're fools.
OBIDA: No more! (*Sound of a big mercedes benz car is heard, with honking in the background. ETHIOPE, as a rich businessman in flowing "agbada" emerges. He walks majestically past the crowd, pulls the Fuel Attendant aside to whisper to him, after which he pushes some currency notes into the Attendant's cupped hand. The women are watching.*)
BENUE: You see? Watch them.
BENUE: What did I tell you?
NIGER: Bribery. It's there.
OBIDA: Always. And they like to hoard and hoard everything.
NIGER: For people wey get money.
OJI/FUEL ATTENDANT (*Aside to the businessman.*): Oga, I hear. Make dem commot first.
ETHIOPE/BUSINESSMAN: I will come back later then?
OJI/FUEL ATTENDANT: Yes saar. Dem too plenty now.
ETHIOPE/BUSINESSMAN: Later then. (*He walks towards the market-place and watches the crowd from that distance .*)
OJI/FUEL/ATTENDANT (*To the crowd.*): You no see the sign? "**No Fuel**". Go away! (*Attendant is irritated and brandishes a sign as Policemen arrive with their whip. They push the crowd backwards. They crowd resists, resumes the banter.*)
NIGER: Dis pickin. No push me-o! I get motor? Na ordinary kalozin me I wan buy-o!
BENUE (*Teasing.*) : Who dash monkey banana?
NIGER: My sister! Who dash monkey? We no kuku get motor.
BENUE: Na common 'kalozin' we wan buy.

NIGER: Na we money too! Dem 'shakara don too much." (*Now angry, the Attendant yanks and pushes them back. NIGER falls down, groaning, but other women help to lift her up again.*)

BENUE: Boy, wetin? You wan kill de poor woman for common patrol?

OJI/FUEL ATTENDANT: So petrol dey common, abi? Why you dey trouble me for am now?

BENUE: I beg, go siddon, o'jare! No kill we-o!

OBIDA (*Still nursing NIGER's bruises.*): Your 'shakara' don too much, self. Afterall na ordinary 'Boy-Boy' you dey do!

OJI/FUEL ATTENDANT (*Incensed, gives them a violent push.*) Me? Houseboy? I go teach you lesson-o!

OBIDA: Go ahead. Let's see... (*Vexed, he starts pulling off his shirt for a fight. Some of them start jeering and cheering him. But the older women try to stop him and he retreats. The Police continue the beat in another direction.*)

OBIDA: Old boy, go open de tin. Just pour your yeye tin and let me go.

OJI/FUEL/ATTENDANT (*To the women.*) : You see now? So na my yeye tin now? (*Pushing them away.*) Oya, make una commot. Commot all of you! (*They resist.*)

NIGER (*Confronting him*): If you touch me again? I go... (*The Attendant retreats, goes behind the fuel pump to produce a koboko whip with which he turns to the crowd.*)

OBIDA (*Daring him.*): Ha! Ha! Ha! Touch am now? If fowl say piss no hard, make e piss am now? (*The Attendant now aims directly at her.*)

OJI/FUEL ATTENDANT (*Threatening.*): Me?

OBIDA: Yes! Wetin? Wetin you be self?

OJI/FUEL ATTENDANT (*Facing OBIDA.*): You wan try me? I go show you-o!

OBIDA: Show me wetin? Wetin you get self wey dey puff your yeye head so?

OJI/FUEL ATTENDANT: No try me-o! Or you go see!

OBIDA: Dare! (*He tries to target OBIDA but the women form a human shield around the girl and block him.*)

BENUE (*Threatening.*): Try de girl now? Touch am!

OBIDA: Touch me wit dat your dead stick. Just go ahead. Strike any woman here with dat your stump and you go smell your head. You common...

NIGER: Attendant!

OBIDA: Who dash am? *Servant*!

BENUE: No be you even get de patrol. Common houseboy.

OJI/FUEL ATTENDANT: Me? Me, houseboy? Don't push me! (*Scuffle. The mob rushes for the pump.*)

OJI/FUEL ATTENDANT (*Struggling and calling out.*): Police! Police!

Somebody call me me de police! Dem go loot am! Petrol! Petrol! Get de petrol...
ETHIOPE/BUSINESSMAN *(Stepping forward.):* Who?
WOMEN *(Teasing.)* Oga, you no hear? E say make we get de petrol *(They rush behind and start pumping the hidden fuel.)*
OJI/FUEL ATTENDANT *(Hysterical.):* Police! Police, oga. Call me de police. Dey wan kill me-o! My oga! Oga go kill me-o! *(The Businessman pulls out cellphone, calls. Soon, KAINJI arrives as the Mobile Police.)*
KAINJI/POLICE: What the hell is going on here?
WOMEN: Shame...pump...
KAINJI/POLICE *(Trying to disperse them with his baton.):* What's the matter with you people?
WOMEN: Petrol!
OJI/FUEL ATTENDANT: No petrol! You deaf?
KAINJI/POLICE *(Pushing them.)* You hear him? Private property. Out! Out!
OJI/FUEL ATTENDANT: Officer, save me. Oga...save me from dis people. My oga go kill me if...
WOMEN: Make he kill you den. Na (h)only we fit to die?
OJI/FUEL /ATTENDANT: You hear dem, Officer?
KAINJI/POLICE *(Dispersing the crowd.):* Clear! Clear all of you. *(Still, they resist. A tug of war, with stampede following as they break through and try to grab the fuel. KOKO as the Seller/Hawker has arrived and entered the struggle to get her share.)*
KOKO *(Excitedly.):* Thank you Lord...
BENUE: Of Patrol!
NIGER: And kalozin! *(They laugh, continue the tug of war with the Fuel Attendant and the Police. The Businessman pulls the Police aside, bribes him. Immediately, the Police pulls out his gun, and mounts guard in front of the pump as the Attendant and the Businessman whisper. Then they both disappear behind the fuel pump.)*
KOKO: You see? You see dem?
WOMEN: Today na today! *(They surge forward, suddenly pushing the Police. The gun falls and they all struggle for it. OBIDA grabs the gun, hands it over to KOKO who aims it at the POLICE while OBIDA charges at the Attendant. Seeing that the Police is now completely overwhelmed and disoriented, the Businessman, wielding his cellphone, starts calling for security reinforcement.)*
BUSINESSMAN: Just wait for the Mobile Police.
WOMEN: Who? Police? *(The women go into a mock drama of the policemen taking bribe.)* 'Woman, wetin you carry? Open, woman! Show me

wetin you carry!'
WOMEN: Make dem come! Come! Come! (*They cheer and jeer, rush at the Police and hold him down.*)
OBIDA: Come now. Ready.
KAINJI/POLICE (*Panting.*): My...my ...gun...You take my gun? Woman, you dey play with fire!
OBIDA: I am fire!
WOMEN: Fire! Fire! We are fire!
NIGER (*Calmly to OBIDA.*): Careful child.
OBIDA: No! Not with these bastards!
WOMEN: Finish am!
OBIDA: All of them!
BENUE: Child, don't. Too much sacrifice.
NIGER: We've lost too much already.
OBIDA: Then let it be.
WOMEN: Show dem! Show dem!
NIGER: There's nothing to show. Animals...
BENUE: Dey play...
OBIDA: With Lions?
WOMEN: Yes, lion! We be lion!
NIGER: Hungry!
BENUE: And angry!
OBIDA: Falling? What do I care? I'm down. Down already? So why should I fear?
BENUE (*Chuckling, calming her down.*): Your head, child. (*She takes the weapon from her.*)
NIGER (*Teasing.*) Sure, she's not lost it already?
BENUE: We've lost too much already.
OBIDA: And so?
BENUE: It matters.
NIGER: Nothing matters...
BENUE: No. Not any more.
NIGER: We get value?
OBIDA: Oh, yes we do! That's why we must show them. Take control of our lives.
WOMEN (*Drumming*): True, daughter. She said it! Show! Show! Show them! Women take control. Take control of our lives! (*Suddenly, the Mobile Police arrives and fires tear-gas into the crowd. Smoke, commotion, as the people are choking and fleeing. KOKO is arrested, handcuffed and pushed into a corner. Meanwhile, OBIDA has broken away from*

the crowd and is yelling: "Attendant! Where's that attendant?" The crowd returns to join her. They find the Attendant getting ready to dispense fuel to the Businessman. OBIDA quickly moves, grabs a container and insists on being served, with other women following and clamoring. "We wan kalozin. We wan fuel. Sell! Sell! Sell us fuel!")

OJI/FUEL ATTENDANT: Women. Trouble...trouble... (*Desperate, he flings OBIDA's container away. She picks it up, returns and replaces it*).

OJI/ATTENDANT: You dey mad?

OBIDA: You too. You're mad. Why? Why give fuel to him and not to us?

OJI/FUEL ATTENDANT: If you wan fuel, den pay...(*Showing*.) Dat na One Thousand....

WOMEN: What?

OJI/FUEL ATTENDANT: Yes. Take it or leave it.

OBIDA: Thief!

WOMEN: Tief! Olleh! Tief! Oshi! Barawo!

OBIDA: Yes. That's how you people hike up everything.

NIGER: So poor people no go get...

OBIDA: You create artificial scarcity.

WOMEN: To cheat us.

BENUE: My pickin! Poor wo...man no get broda!

OBIDA: Yes, my people. Failure is an orphan.

OJI/FUEL ATTENDANT: Yes. You say you be sometin? Pay now. Time to show say you be sometin.

OBIDA: Yes, I am. Somebody.

WOMEN: A teacher!

OJI/FUEL ATTENDANT (*Mock laughter.*) So you be *teasha*? Ordinary teasha dey make all dis wahala since? Ha, teasha! Wetin you sabi? You empty pocket!

OBIDA: Wretched thing!

OJI/ATTENDANT (*Laughing*): See you! See am! See who dey call person wretched. Government don pay you for so many months? You jobless...

OBIDA: Is it your business?

OJI/FUEL ATTENDANT (*Teasing, dancing.*): Ha, teasha. So-so gbese... debt...full here, full dere. No wonder body dey pain you. Ha! Pepper Eye! Hungry woman. Look him face. Monkey zoo. Na wetin do your face? Ohooo! Cockroach! Na cockroach lick him face. (*He laughs and teases. OBIDA's now more incensed and confronts the Businessman.*).

OBIDA: It's people like you who turn this country upside down.

ETHIOPE/BUSINESSMAN: Woman, go away! I have no business with you.

OBIDA: Oh, yes you do. Why must you bribe your way through everything?

ETHIOPE/BUSINESSMAN (*Arrogantly.*) Am I in your way?
OBIDA: Yes, you are! All of you, wrecking us with your ill-gotten wealth.
ETHIOPE/BUSINESSMAN: You are just jealous.
OBIDA: Of you? For what?
CROWD (*Jeering and cheering*): Yes! Tell am! Curse am!
ETHIOPE/BUSINESSMAN: Frustrated old maid! Go find yourself a husband!
OBIDA: Certainly not your type!
ETHIOPE/ BUSINESSMAN: What would I do with a thing like you?
OBIDA: When the time comes, you'd wish you had this *thing* like me.
ETHIOPE/BUSINESSMAN: Hear her? Your type? Never! Never have any dealing with your type, woman! You must be dreaming.
OBIDA: And I'll wake up. Yes we must. Just wait. Time is...
ETHIOPE/BUSINESSMAN (*Laughing.*) What time?
WOMEN: You'll see.
ETHIOPE/BUSINESSMAN: Ah, women! And time? Oh well, nothing new.
WOMEN: You'll see.
ETHIOPE/BUSINESSMAN: If you say so. (*Pause.*) But I know...We'll take it...whatever comes...We'll be ready.
OBIDA: When judgment comes?
ETHIOPE/BUSINESSMAN (*Laughing in her face.*): Dreamer! You wish!
WOMEN: Are you ready then? Repent! Repent! Jesus is coming back for him world!
ETHIOPE/BUSINESSMAN: These charlatans! Driving everyone crazy with their religious...antics. Nonsense! What's this country coming to? Won't let one sleep or rest. In traffic, marketplace, churches, stores, everywhere. Swarm of fleas buzzing in your ear. (*Parodying.*) Repent! Repent! Change! Jesus saves! Jesus is coming! Repent! Jesus is coming to where?
OBIDA (*Taunting him.*): Here, to get you! Make your dirty mouth bleed. (*He yanks her. OBIDA falls, rises and braces up for a fight. The crowd continues cheering and jeering.*)
ATTENDANT: Do your worse now. (*Calls back the police.*)
POLICE (*Returning.*): Na wetin? Man no go rest? Leave me o'jare! I tire!
CROWD: I tire no be lazy! Ha! Ha! Ha! (*He steps behind. They rush into the station, overpower the Fuel Attendant and loot the fuel and kerosene.*)
ETHIOPE/BUSINESSMAN: Don't worry. I've called for more security reinforcement.
CROWD (*Laughing.*): Quick, quick, make you call dem. No to you start am?
ETHIOPE/BUSINESSMAN (*Spiteful look at OBIDA*): It's all her fault. That

witch. You think you can get away with this?
OBIBA (*Threatening*): Don't try me-o! (*KAINJI as the Mobile Police returns.*)
CROWD (*Shouting.*) : Na operation sweep-o! Run! Run! (*Crowd fleas.*)
ETHIOPE/BUSINESSMAN (*To Police.*): That's the criminal!
POLICE (*Grabbing NIGER.*): This one?
ETHIOPE/BUSINESSMAN: No. De one behind wey him face be like Ekpo...mask Miss Ugly...She started it all. (*Police makes a dash for OBIDA who tries to flee.*)
POLICE: Halt!
OBIDA: Why? What for?
POLICE: You've been arrested Under Section 10. Subsection 36458 of the Penal Code law.
OBIDA: Nonsense!
POLICE: What? Me? Nonsense? (*He grabs her*).
OBIDA: Leave me alone. I'm innocent. That's the man you should arrest.
(*The Police slaps her. Her face is bleeding as she's being handcuffed.*)
ETHIOPE/BUSINESSMAN (*Mocking OBIDA.*): You think this is a jungle? A lawless country where you can just run your filthy mouth anyhow? Well, now you know. This fucking country does have some law and order! Ha! Ha! Ha! (*Exit Businessman. Sounds of his Rolls Royce blasting off. OBIDA kicks and curses as she is being dragged away. As soon as Businessman leaves, the women start pleading for the girls in custody.*)
NIGER: I beg. Make you lef am.
BENUE: Na my friend pickin be dat.
POLICE (*Ignoring them.*): And den?
NIGER: I beg.
POLICE: Na beg-beg I go chop? (*Aside, NIGER and BENUE confer, produce some roasted corn which they offer to the Police. Indignant, the Police starts walking away but the women continue pleading.*)
POLICE: You mean say I be cheap article wey you fit buy wit...wit...nonsense...chaff? (*Mock laughter.*) Ha, country! Police don see somtin for naija! Ha! Police don turn to article without value. (*Sternly.*) Look, here woman. You see dis uniform? E be like wetin you fit buy wit... wit...corn?
NIGER (*Pleading, adding some currency notes.*): I beg. Take. Na de only tin we get to chop we give you so.
BENUE (*Passionately.*): I swear. God dey hear we. Na de only tin we get be dat. I beg.
POLICE: So that is all?

NIGER and BENUE: Everything. All we get. (*Police stares at them briefly, then slowly starts leaning to take his prize.*)
POLICE: God knows I'm hungry too.
NIGER & BENUE: Like we dey too! Plenty plenty of we! Hunger! Hunger dey wire we head!
POLICE: For three months, dem never pay us.
NIGER: So de government expect you to work for empty stomach?
POLICE: Bring am my sista. (*Takes the corn and eats greedily.*): Dem say "half bread beta pass noting."
NIGER & BENUE: True-true my broda! Half bread beta pass notin.
POLICE (*Mouthful.*) Hnm...my sistah. Tell me how man for do! (*They laugh as he chews greedily.*) Work-work, no pay. How monkey go dey work, baboon go dey chop? Ehn?
POLICE: And you hear de president? (*Parodying, play-acting.*) 'Fellow Nai...Hungerians! Hard times ahead! So tighten your belt!" (*Laughter.*)
NIGER & BENUE (*Mimicking.*): Even when E dey untie him own? (*More laughter.*)
POLICE: My sista. Dat na special brand of Najia Justice.
NIGER & BENUE: Na so we see-am-o! (*Police releases KOKO.*)
POLICE (*Bites deeply into the corn husk.*): And dis na my own special brand! Ha! Ha! Ha!
NIGER: I beg, my broda. Don't forget dat we other small sistah.
POLICE: Dat one?
BENUE: Yes-o, my broda. Make you forgive am.
POLICE: I see-am. E too make trouble.
NIGER: Lef am. Na small pickin.
POLICE: E still dey wash him belle? (*They laugh.*)
WOMEN: True-true! E no sabi anytin. I beg lef am for us.
POLICE: Ok ay-o! As you talk. Me I go tell de sergeant to lef am...say una don pay.
WOMEN: Our broda! Thank you-o!!! (*POLICE studies the girl for a while, then he releases her as he speaks.*) You self, you too make trouble. Proper *gba-gba-ti* girl you be! You too sabi. (*Sternly.*) Now look here. If you ever enter trouble again, I no go save you-o! Go now and behave yourself. Go home woman! Your faith has saved you. No be so de church people dey talk am? Tomorrow is another day. (*He drinks, belches, and starts picking at his teeth.*). Me, I don belle full...
NIGER & BENUE: No. You belle-wise!
POLICE: Yes, my people. (*Emphatically.*) Belle-Wise! Wetin concern agbero

wit overload? Ha! Ha! Ha! (*Belches, hiccups, loudly.*) Who say I never do my job? Country can go to blazes! Ha! Ha! Ha! Go home, women. The men and chidren are waiting.

NIGER: For dem grave...

POLICE: Dem kill your own too? (*NIGER nods, sighs.*)

NIGER: Yes. Just for dat protest.

BENUE: And my own too.

POLICE: Bloody....

OBIDA: Country.

POLICE: Waste. Bloody waste. (*Pensive.*) Just go and rest. Too risky here.
(*He whistles, turns businesslike again, and starts walking as he sees the others coming.*)

WOMEN (*Departing.*): Thank you! Thank you! Oga!

POLICE: No problem. I dey for your side. Poor man no get broda.

WOMEN: Yes, broda. Failure is an orphan.

POLICE (*To the girls.*) : You know where I am. Call me whenever you need me.

ALL THE WOMEN: We will. Thank you.

(*Exit Police. Light dims. Everyone now hurries home.*)

# MOVEMENT FOUR

*( Twilight. The market-square is empty except for OBIDA in combat attire. She crosses, pacing up and down between the market-place and the locked GRA/Oil Club. She's talking to herself as she displays some protest literature not far from the gate of the GRA/Oil Club. KOKO as the Seller/Hawker, soon appears with her fruit basket (bananas, oranges and pineapples delicately balanced on her head. She looks exhausted, but graceful and dignified in her slow march to the GRA Oil Club with her usual chants and erotic steps.)*

HAWKER/KOKO: Buy my orange! Buy banana! Sweet sweet pineapple! (*No response. Her chanting gets more desperate.*) Buy my orange banana, pineapple! Na de sweetest juice in the world!

OBIDA (*Jokingly.*): Old girl, you no dey tire?

HAWKER/KOKO: Do I have a choice?

OBIDA: Go home, my friend. Those people have more than enough juices to last them a life time. (*OBIDA improvises her new anthem or National Pledge, which she recites with KOKO.*)

OBIDA: I pledge to Hungeria my country.

KOKO: To be faithful, loyal and (ho)nest.

KOKO: To serve Hungeria with all my strength.

KOKO: To defend her unity and honor.

OBIDA (*Loudly.*): SOLD!

KOKO: Sold-Sold-Sold-Sold!

OBIDA: So help me..

KOKO: God! And wish me...

OBIDA: Luck. Amen! (*Pause.*) Long live!

KOKO: Hungeria!! (*OBIDA stands at attention, gives military salute and resumes her new National Pledge. Sudden commotion; people running and being pursued by others. The runners are OSHUN and KAINJI NIGER and BENUE. NIGER and BENUE are in pursuit.*)

NIGER (*Desperately.*): Who dey dere? I beg. Holl-am! Holl-am for me!

BENUE: I beg. My son. Come back. (*The fugitives quicken their pace. OSHUN's dressed to kill in her short, hot-pants. KAINJI now as the Bandit-Boy is in his baggy trousers, t-shirt and base-ball cap.*)

NIGER (*Panting.*): Holl am!

KOKO & OBIDA: Who?

NIGER: De gal. My daughter. Lost. (*OSHUN dribbles her as she pursues. NIGER misses a step, stumbles and stops to catch her breath. BENUE assists her as she too cries out for help look help. The teenagers turn to romance and tease the women, who look helpless. OBIDA and KOKO struggle to help the mothers block the way. But then voices of other youths are encouraging the fugitives with cheers.)*

NIGER: Is there nobody ready to help a tired woman? Helepu! Helepu meeee-o!

OSHUN: Don't touch me!

KAINJI: Don't touch me-o! *(Moves to block their assailants. Meanwhile, OBIDA tries to restrain NIGER and BENUE from the chase.)*

NIGER: Hollaaaaaam!!

VOICES OF YOUTHS: Go. Ride on!

WOMEN: Stop, children! Children stop!

VOICES OF YOUTHS: Don't stop! Keep moving! These parents!

WOMEN: Children!

VOICES OF YOUTHS: These parents! Parents! Parents! What can they do anyway? What do they want?

WOMEN: Keep you out of trouble.

OSHUN: But we *are* trouble.

OJI: Yes. So how can anyone keep us away from *us*?

VOICES OF YOUTHS: Keep us prisoners at home.

WOMEN: Safety. Your safety!

VOICES OF YOUTHS: Really? Can they afford it?

OSHUN & OJI: Can they afford anything?

VOICES OF YOUTHS: Our parents. Wretched wretched and poor.

OSHUN & OJI: Tired, wretched...

VOICES OF YOUTHS *(Chanting.)*: Poor ...poorer...poorest! Go girl! We dig your style. We won't yield! No won't yield! We're following in your footsteps! *(The youths break into rap music and dance, which the fugitive pair gladly lead as they swing dance and hold onto each other seductively. The parents watch in absolute dismay.)*

BENUE: *(Sighing.):* What is our world turning to?

OSHUN *(Smiling, flexing muscles.)*: Youths!

KAINJI & OSHUN: Yeah. Yeah! We got the power! More power to the youths! *(They laugh.)*

NIGER *(To the women)*: My sistah. See me see trouble-o! *(The women are in shock and remain silent. KOKO exits in anger. NIGER takes out something from her bra. Then she approaches her daughter OSHUN . BENUE too takes out a similar thing from her own bra as she approaches the defiant couple.)*

BENUE: Come. Come home.

KAINJI: Where is the home?

BENUE: I know (*Choking.*) I know it's nothing but it's ours.
KAINJI: Then stay there. I won't (*Emphatically.*) I will not! (*He swings and does an erotic jig with OSHUN.*)
OSHUN: You mothers leave us alone to fend for ourselves. Can't you see we're ready to go?
NIGER (*Pleading with her daughter.*): Then take it, my daughter. Rich or poor, I want you alive; not dead.
OSHUN (*Curious.*): What is that?
NIGER: You know. Raincoat..
BENUE (*Irritated.*): Condom. Not raincoat. Let's name it right. Call it what it is. These children need to get the point. Protection! Protection! Protection! (*The defiant pair laugh loud, with voices of the other youths magnifying their laughter.*)
KAINJI/OSHUN: These parents must be running out of ideas. You think we know nothing?
BENUE: And Aids too is out there...
NIGER: With unwanted babies calling!
WOMEN (*Chanting.*): Oh, so many-so many many troubles calling our youths!
NIGER: It's raining.
BENUE: It's wet.
NIGER: Slippery. It's life. Tough.
BENUE: And rough.
WOMEN: Children you must arm yourselves with raincoats in the rainy...
BENUE: Stormy weather.
KAINJI/OSHUN (*In a sing-song manner*): No, we won't.
WOMEN: Oh yes, you will!
OSHUN: What for?
KAINJI: You know you're losing anyway.
NIGER: But see, children? What you have, you hold!
BENUE: Protect...
WOMEN: Protection! Protection! Protection!
KAINJI & OSHUN: And you think we don't know?
NIGER: Well, nobody says you don't.
BENUE: And you think you know more than we do?
NIGER: Yes. That's kids nowadays. They think they know more than their parents.
KAINJI/OSHUN (*Taunting.*): And we do? Doubt it?
   (*Again, they swing and break into erotic dance-steps*).
KAINJI: You doubt it? That's where we're going.

OSHUN: To the GRA/ Oil Club!
KAINJI: To arm ourselves.
OSHUN: By hook or crook.
NIGER: And get killed?
BENUE: Or jailed?
KAINJI: It doesn't matter.
OSHUN: Nothing matters.
KAINJI: Anymore. (*Silence.*) And if we don't go? Can you feed...
OSHUN: Fend for us?
KAINJI: Send us to school?
OSHUN: Give us employment?
KAINJI: Buy our clothing?
OSHUN: Provide all our needs?
KAINJI: So what choices have we got?
OSHUN: But only to take destiny into our hands. (*As they speak, the women watch helplessly.*)
BENUE (*Tearfully.*): Son, the "hell" people don't joke...
KAINJI: Shame!
BENUE: Yes. They'll kill you...anybody in their way.
KAINJI (*Beating his chest.*): Let them try!
BENUE: You know they will.
KAINJI: Then it's my lot.
NIGER: No, it's not. You're taking the law into your own hands.
OSHUN: So?
KAINJI: It's her life.
OSHUN (*Strutting.*): It's my life.
NIGER: Then take it.
BENUE: They'll kill you.
OSHUN: Whatever. I'm going!
KAINJI: To teach those bas... (*Swiftly, he grabs OSHUN. With the voices of youths still cheering and blasting the air with their rap music even louder, the rebellious pair does some final erotic dance-steps together and run toward the gate of the GRA/OIL Club. For a while after their departure, the women stare helplessly at one another, until NIGER breaks into a somber tune which the other women join.*)
BENUE (*Subdued.*): Sad.
NIGER: Very sad. What can we do?
OBIDA: Something's got to be done.
NIGER: How?
BENUE (*Voice cracking.*) How...? Sisters, we're losing.

OBIDA: And violated! Didn't I tell you about my own experience? (*Sobs.*) They ate me... raw...(*Sobbing.*)
NIGER: Yes. Losing on all sides.
BENUE: Losing our sons.
NIGER: Our daughters.
BENUE: Losing brothers...sisters.
WOMEN: Losing! Losing! Losing...on all sides... Everything.
OBIDA: Mothers, we've got to do something! Something.
NIGER: She's said it. Said it!
BENUE: She's said it! (*They stretch their hands, link up and spread across the road. Now the women have formed a human shield across the road in the marketplace.*)
OBIDA: From now on, nobody goes through the marketplace without us.
BENUE (*Firmly.*): From now on, nobody passes any road without us.
OBIDA: We are together.
WOMEN: Together! Together! Together! Women stay together!
OBIDA (*Excitedly calling.*): Mothers!
WOMEN: Eeeeh!
OBIDA: Who owns this land?
WOMEN: We own this land!
OBIDA: Who spoils this land?
WOMEN: We spoil this land.
OBIDA: Who sweeps this land?
WOMEN: We sweep the land!
OBIDA: Who seals this land?
WOMEN: We seal the land.
OBIDA: Who heals the wounds?
WOMEN: We... (*They are still madly absorbed in this incantatory chant when the Seller/Hawker KOKO returns wailing as she runs back from the GRA/OIL Club gate.*)
NIGER: Oh I'm dead, my daughter! (*Chasing KOKO.*)
WOMEN: Another daughter.
NIGER (*Pleading.*): Tell me what is wrong? What did they do to you? (*KOKO ignores her mother and continues hastily and tearfully on her journey home.*)
NIGER: Somebody help! Help! That's the only one I have left. And now I'm losing her too? (*The women try to stop KOKO but she pushes her way through and marches on.*)
KOKO: Leave me alone, everybody, I'm tired. Tired, I too I'm ready now to find my own way!

OBIDA (*Thrusts herself on the road to block KOKO.*) Come with me. Where is the fruit? (*KOKO sobs.*)
OBIDA: Gone? They took it? (*KOKO nods.*)
OBIDA: Ah, I know they do. You too, raped? (*Silence.*)
NIGER (*Hysterical.*): Whooooooooo? Who dares touch my daughter?
BENUE: Who dares-who dares! Daughter of the land-Daughter of the sea!
OBIDA: They did it-did it. Yes they did! (*More sobbing* from KOKO.)
BENUE: The soldiers? (*At this point, KOKO explodes into tears. The women encircle her as she weeps silently. But with each question, she nods her head.*)
WOMEN (*Stunned.*): Soldiers? Police?
NIGER (*Choking with tears.*): B...bu... they were sent here to pro...tect us?
BENUE: You think it matters to them?
NIGER: Is it the white man? (*Silence.*)
BENUE: The government official?
OBIDA: Or the Chief? (*KOKO weeps louder. OBIDA comforts her.*)
KOKO (*Tearfully*): All...all of them. Cut deep with their knife. I fought. Tried...tried to close my eyes. Tight. (*Screams.*) Aaah! How I prayed God to close them forever. Bury me, alive. But when I opened, I saw him...grinning...grinning into my face. The Thief...(*Screams.*) Aaaaaah! God, now I know...You? Man? Why did you do this to me? Why? True? God? (*Sing-song.*) What...what are you? Where? Where are you? (*The women hold her as she falls.*)
NIGER: Child. Know you're not alone. (*KOKO breaks away from the women but OBIDA persists.*)
NIGER (*Frustrated.*): Are they never tired of ruining...?
OBIDA: Killing us!
BENUE: At Odi?
WOMEN: They raped and killed women!
NIGER: In Choba?
WOMEN: They raped and killed women!
BENUE: Across the sea?
WOMEN: They raped and killed women.
NIGER: In the land?
WOMEN: They raped...tore up...aaaaaaah!
BENUE: And still...
WOMEN: They're raping, selling and killing us.
KOKO (*Exploding.*) Mother I tell you. I won't go there anymore. But you keep pushing, pushing me to go...
NIGER: To sell. Yes. It's my fault. But child, what could I do? We had nothing.

Nothing to eat.
KOKO: But you let her, your daughter OSHUN run to those foreigners...
NIGER: She is selling too, daughter. She says she has to sell ...what she has.
KOKO (*Stripping her clothes*): Am I the one to be left out? I too have to sell what I got. See? Mother see? I'm tired. I too can sell. (*She gets hysterical, dances provocatively.*) And sell I will! It's easier, much easier if you let me go? What more have you got to lose?
NIGER (*Holding her.*): You, my daughter!
KOKO (*Laughing.*): I too have got to go.
NIGER: Daughter, do it for me. Please!
KOKO: I said I won't. Now, I too I'm going. Yes. As they say, if you can't beat them, join them! (*Pause.*) Five years out of school. Robbed of life. Robbed...of dignity. And what have I become? A petty trader. Yes. That's all. Is that all I should be about? Is that? No. I know I'm worth more. Much more than they're willing to buy or pay for. And now I say no. I too I'm fixing my own price. (*Deliberately.*) I am going to Europe...to Italy where the business is hot...and I too will sell like hotcake. He said it, the great Thief...I mean the Chief, our leader.. (*Strutting.*) Yes, I'm gonna cash in on my own luck. (*OBIDA follows and pleads with KOKO, pulls her aside.*)
OBIDA: Don't. Don't go. Let's stay here. Work it out together in our home...
KOKO: This is no home.
OBIDA: But it is ours.
KOKO: Yes, ours. Taken. Taken! The nation? Prostitutes...Look, if this is our land, who rules it? (*Screams.*) Foreigners! Strangers! Who controls it? Do we have a voice? Do we? How can we be in our own homes and be so afraid? Are we not the strangers...strangers in our own land? (*Pause.*) Now hear this. (*She quickly pulls out the admission offers she received from the University, and reads*).
FROM: Director of Undergraduate Admissions
National University
Naija State.
Hungeria
November 20, 1998.
Dear Ms. KOKO Atiene,
*It's with great pleasure that I offer you admission to the Department of Law in this great citadel of learning. In accepting this offer, you will be joining students and staff with world renowned potentials and credentials. The deadline for you to secure your admission is December 1, 19... To ensure your place, you must deposit a non*

refundable fee of 10,000.00 Naija cash to the university Bursar. Thereafter, you are expected to report for orientation and classes on December 8 at our Pipeline Campus auditorium. We look forward to your participation in our rich, rigorous campus life.
Congratulations!
Signed,
All-you-want,
Registrar of National University.
(After reading the letter aloud, KOKO holds it up, shouts to the women.)
KOKO: And mother, what is today's date? Ha! Years after, after my deadline and I'm still here. Searching... Searching for the deposit to...to...my life. Yes. (Shakes her buttocks vigorously.) Here it is. My insurance for tomorrow. Ha! Ha! Ha! (Laughing, she steps towards her mother, tears the letter right in her mother's face and throws it into the air like confetti.)
KOKO (Laughing.): There goes the dream! For one...two...three...four...five.... five years... Five good years of my youth, I struggled, studied and suffered to get admitted into the university. What use is it now? What use? (Hysterical.) All those thousands and millions of educated youth who struggled to gain the education and find jobs? Where are they now? Where are the jobs? Where are the youths? On the streets! In graves or jails! Mother, I too am tired. I'm taking the easy way out. I'm joining my sister. Yes OSHUN! She tells me the foreigner is taking her to Italy or some other European city. I too am going! (She turns her back, starts running.)
OBIDA (Chasing.): The West. Weired place! Don't go. No! Oh no please! Don't. In the name of everything you cherish. Don't! They'll ruin you there. They'll wreck you, turn you to prost...
KOKO: Yes, make money. Cash. Hard, hard, currency. That is what speaks.
OBIDA (Desperate.): Bloody. They'll get a dog to...to...Oh no, don't you see? Look at me. My own uncle gave me to the foreigner who gave me to...to...His dog? (Screams.) Aya ya ya yaaaah! (BENUE steps in and holds OBIDA back, knowing how emotional she can get when she speaks about her own experience.)
BENUE: Listen. Listen to her, child. (KOKO's silent for a while, until she breaks into a familiar blues tune.)
WOMEN: Listen, child.
NIGER: Daughter, hear me.
WOMEN: Hear her. Listen. Child, listen to your mother!
OBIDA (Exploding.): The selling...

WOMEN: Must be stopped!
OBIDA: The raping...
WOMEN: Must be stopped!
OBIDA: The killing...
WOMEN: Must be stopped!
OBIDA: The profiteering...
WOMEN: Must be stopped!
OBIDA: The corruption...
WOMEN: Must be stopped!
BENUE: Women. This is our fight...
NIGER: Together! This is *our* fight!
OBIDA: Yes, she said it!
KOKO: Said it-Said it-Said it!
WOMEN: Yes, she said it!
KOKO: So mothers. When do we meet?
WOMEN: Tomorrow!
OBIDA: Yes, tomorrow.
KOKO: We'll march.
WOMEN: March! March! March! (*With KOKO at the center, all the women dance and march toward the GRA/OIL Club until the lights fade into the next stage.*)

# MOVEMENT FIVE

(*ATLANTIC, alone. He is smoking in the lounge area when OJI as his clergy-friend joins him. Soon after, OSHUN appears at the gate. ATLANTIC is obviously uneasy for he would like to let her in but can't because of his important guest.*)

OJI/PRIEST: So you know her?
ATLANTIC (*Pretending.*): Can't see that far now.
OJI PRIEST: You do.
ATLANTIC (*Fidgeting.*): Ehnm... No...Ehmmm.. Used to...You know...One of those cooks, maybe?
OJI/PRIEST: I see. Just be careful.
OJI/PRIEST: So I see. But know, that's a very loose one.
ATLANTIC (*Jokingly.*) A loose canon you mean? (*As their conversation develops, actual voices of the protesters rise slowly in the background. ATLANTIC listens, sighs, "Oh nothing significant. We'll teach them. They'll have to learn." He waves off the concern and motions to OJI to resume their chat. OSHUN, too, is temporarily out of sight as she follows the direction of the rising mob action. OSHUN reappears again as suddenly as she had disappeared.*)
OJI/PRIEST: Whatever. But I'd say steer clear. (*Sighing.*) Women? These times?
ATLANTIC: And in these parts?
OJI/PRIEST: Native women. Hnm...They've changed a lot. Used to be a lot different.
ATLANTIC: Really?
OJI/PRIEST: Yes. (*Counting.*) Ten whole years. I've been here long enough to know the difference.
ATLANTIC: Wao! (*Laughing, crossing over to peep through and to unlock the gate.*) And they haven't offered you a Chieftaincy title yet?
OJI/PRIEST: Not quite. But they try...
ATLANTIC: Quite unlike them. These people. Used to open policies. Always ready for...
OJI/PRIEST: Aids?
ATLANTIC: That too. They're always willing to give up anything.
OJI/PRIEST: But as a good Christian, you must hold up your head above these natives at all times.
ATLANTIC: Father, don't I know it? (*Rising mob chants. They listen.*)

OJI/PRIEST: Well, just thought I'd remind you. It's getting too hot here. *(He sees the restless OSHUN reappear at the gate, then sighs.)* These natives! Aaaah!
ATLANTIC: I know. *(Pause, puffs at his cigar.)* Except we still have to depend... I mean who else would do all these bloody chores?
OJI/PRIEST *(Pours himself a drink.)*: Just be careful. *Brethren, know thyself.* That's all.
ATLANTIC: I'm completely in control.
OJI/PRIEST *(Rising.):* You should. *(Pause.)* But you know her?
ATLANTIC: Hnm...yes...no *(Pause.)* A domestic help, maybe?
OSHUN *(Hearing this, OSHUN storms into the scene and brandishes a wristwatch ATLANTIC's face.)* Oga, you left this inside. When you came last night.
ATLANTIC *(Stretching to take it but she pulls back.)*: Oh my God. The room!
OSHUN: *My* room.
ATLANTIC: You may keep it. For now. *(OSHUN drops the watch back in her bag. Silence as ATLANTIC tries eyeballing and signaling her to leave until the road is clear but, so determined to assert her presence, OSHUN stands in his face. The Priest is scandalized and looks away. Silence, but for ATLANTIC's whistling. Then OSHUN again breaks the silence.)*
OSHUN *(To ATLANTIC)*: Oga, I've come. Anything else you want from me?
ATLANTIC *(Relieved, jumps.)* What do you have to offer?
OSHUN *(Bluffing)*: Beer? Bloody Mary? Gin and lime? Whisky? Brandy? All on the rocks!
ATLANTIC: Hmn...I'll have the Bloody Mary. *(Fanning himself.)* Too hot in here. *(Turns to the Priest.)* Take something, my friend.
OJI/PRIEST: No. Thanks. I'm fine.
ATLANTIC *(Insisting.)* Come on, Father. Have a beer? Some Bloody Mary?
OSHUN *(To the Priest.)*: Father, I've got everything you need.
OJI/PRIEST: No, thanks.
ATLANTIC: Soft drinks? Iced tea? Egg nog? Bournvita?
OJI/PRIEST: Ok. Ordinary tea will do.
OSHUN: Yes, Father. *(She exists through the door behind ATLANTIC and soon returns with a* tray-full of drinks*, glasses, a boiling tea kettle, with a cup. With her backside in ATLANTIC's direction, she bends to serve the Priest, first.)*
OSHUN *(Pouring the hot tea)*: Father. Like some milk?
OJI/PRIEST: Yes. Thanks.
OSHUN *(Pours the milk.)* And sugar?

OJI/PRIEST: Sure!
OSHUN: I thought so. (*She quickly dips her hand into her bra, and produces two cubes of sugar.*)
OJI/PRIEST (*Stunned.*) What?
OSHUN (*Smiling.*): Father, you like it sweet. Don't you?
OJI/PRIEST (*Scandalized.*): Yes... Oh..but... Not now. Not any more. Thanks.
OSHUN: Father, welcome to Africa!
ATLANTIC (*Laughing.*): These women! (*The Priest rises.*) I should be going now.
OSHUN (*Pleading.*): Father, stay. If you don't like this one, you can have another...
OJI/PRIEST: No thanks. Some other time, maybe. (*Turning to ATLANTIC who's still so amused.*) I must be going now. And remember I'll be be going back to Europe soon.
ATLANTIC: Me too. When are you leaving?
OJI/PRIEST: Next week.
ATLANTIC: So soon?
OJI/PRIEST: Well, about time. It does get lonely out here. And with your deputy in the off-shore fields? My friend, take care.
ATLANTIC: It does really get lonely. I know. (*ATLANTIC escorts his guest to the gate. OSHUN waves him good-bye and returns to the inner chamber.*)
OJI: May God be with you, and guide you.
ATLANTIC: Amen. I know He will. Always! (*OJI/Priest departs. OSHUN too, returns to gather the empty glasses. ATLANTIC trails her loaded chest with his hawkish eyes as he pokes her with a long cigar and nudges her to light it for him. Meanwhile, KOKO as the Seller/Hawker again appears at the gate with her fruits and chants. Their mother, NIGER soon joins her, together with BENUE and KAINJI as an unemployed youth, begging and pleading at the gate for employment. ATLANTIC is so irritated by their noise, he yells at them: 'No vacancy. Out! Out of the premises!' But they still plead. Frustrated, ATLANTIC yells: 'Are you deaf? I said no vacancy!' But still they plead their cause. Vexed, ATLANTIC rises as he threatens: 'Ok, now, I'll deal with you.' At that point, the people begin to hurry out. OSHUN, who stands, frozen and silently watching this development suddenly, drops the tray of glasses which come crashing down at her feet and ATLANTIC's. For a moment they both stand staring at the broken pieces until their eyes meet and OSHUN bends down to pick up the pieces, with ATLANTIC absorbed in his thoughts and*

*watching her until he reaches out to her, holds her tenderly and tries to reassure her with a familiar melody. But OSHUN is lost in thought in her own world. She stares at him, coldly.)*

ATLANTIC *(Kissing her.):* Troubled, girl? *(OSHUN, silent and distracted.)* Fear not, says the Lord for I am thy Lord and thy God. And I will be with you till the very end. Just lay your trust in me.

OSHUN *(Rising.)* You know what my mother told me?

ATLANTIC: Tell me, Babe. What did your Mama say?

OSHUN: 'Trust no man.'

ATLANTIC *(Pulling her down.):* Even me? All men are not the same.

OSHUN: Not equal. *(KAINJI as The Government Official enters the scene.)*

ATLANTIC: And in the eyes of God?

KAINJI: He knows better.

OSHUN: Oga, why don't you just leave God out of it? *(ATLANTIC is attempting to kiss and fondle again but OSHUN is already on her feet, facing the room behind them.)*

OSHUN: I'm hungry.

ATLANTIC: For God?

OSHUN *(Playfully, and picking up the tray.)* Are you? You take too much.

KAINJI: Man's lot. Take care, young woman. And be fast. I know your mother...

OSHUN: Is waiting. Won't be long now. *(Laughs loud and exists into the room.)*

KAINJI: Good luck. *(Turning to ATLANTIC.)* Now don't forget tomorrow. Our business...

ATLANTIC: Hell no! How can I forget. The business is our life.

KAINJI: To control.

ATLANTIC: I'm ready.

KAINJI: Always. And that's why I'm here. We have a lot to share, you and I.

ATLANTIC: True.

KAINJI: And that is why we must take care of ourselves, first.

*(He pulls his chair closer to ATLANTIC.)*

KAINJI: You know that man is...is funny?

ATLANTIC: Which man?

KAINJI: The Chief, you know.

ATLANTIC *(Scribbling at a sign-post.):* Hmmm...Oh yes! Oh, yes!

KAINJI: You trust him?

ATLANTIC: Hnm...?

KAINJI: You do.

ATLANTIC *(Pretending.):* What?

KAINJI: I say do you trust the chief?

ATLANTIC *(Smiling.):* Oh that? *(Hesitates.)* Yeah, as much as the weather.
KAINJI: Oh come on, you seem to him like a lot. Do a lot of business with him.
ATLANTIC: Do I have a choice? He's the traditional thief...Pardon, Chief. *(Pause.)* And by the way, where's that gypsy?
KAINJI: The girl?
ATLANTIC: The boy. The guard.
    *(He presses the button by his side. No response. Repeats. No response.)*
ATLANTIC: Monkeying around, probably.
KAINJI: Or sleeping.
ATLANTIC: You know them. Always sleeping on the job. *(Peeps into the security post.)*
KAINJI: Not in his place?
ATLANTIC: He's gone. *(Sighs.)* These black...Oh Boy! Always the same response. *(Mimicking.)* "Sir he's not on seat-not on seat" When will they ever be on heat?
KAINJI: Seat! *(Chuckles.)*
ATLANTIC: Whatever!
KAINJI: Never. *(Pause.)* And that girl too. I know how you feel. Ehm...ehm..I don't want to get into your business. But, be careful. None of these people can be trusted.
ATLANTIC *(Loud laughter)*: You telling me? Of course I know. Can't you see I'm always checking? *(Steals glances at the Government Official who is digging the ground to mount the post.)*
KAINJI: I don't blame you. It's too risky.
ATLANTIC: Yes. Here. Too risky to trust.
KAINJI: But it's all part of it. *(Silence.)* But trust me, I have a special offer. Let's make a deal. *(Stunned, ATLANTIC stares at him. Silence.)*
KAINJI: You know the new offshore line? *(Silence.)*
ATLANTIC *(Suspicious.)*: Hmn...Yes.
KAINJI: We can make a fortune...you and me...
ATLANTIC: What?
KAINJI *(Smiling.):* Pump a million barrels or more a day. No records. Ships waiting at sea. Sale sealed. Paid in dollars or pound sterling overseas into your account and mine. No hassles. Just that we'll have to displace more villagers.
ATLANTIC *(Animated.)*: Easily!
KANJI: Yes.
ATLANTIC: Order them to move out...to...to...But where to?

KAINJI: I know. The camp is bursting full. And there's been no running water for one year. No light and other amenities either.
ATLANTIC: Diseased. A cesspool of epidemics.
KAINJI: Cholera gains...
ATLANTIC: Well, we can't help it. They'll have to figure it out by themselves.
KAINJI: One way or the other.
ATLANTIC: Right! (*Pause.*) But honestly, your idea sounds good to me.
KAINJI: Really?
ATLANTIC: Great.
KAINJI (*Exuberantly.*): Think. You and I work for governments...for companies. We're not getting younger, you know? Time passes. Daily we're working our butts off. At home we have a saying that the horn-blower also has the need to blow his nose. Yes! (*ATLANTIC smiles.*) Government company pays itself. We, too, must learn to pay ourselves. First. (*Watching to let the idea sink in.*)
ATLANTIC: (*Hesitating.*) Hnm...makes sense... And why not? Great.. Sounds like a good idea. (*Pause.*) One thing, though. I don't trust...I mean...feel safe with anyone...I mean...Can't you see the look of hate in these people's eyes? Even the domestic servants who work for you!
KAINJI: I know what you mean. In our position we can't ever be too careful.
ATLANTIC: I'm glad you understand. The tone is changing here. It used to be much more comfortable. But these days. These youths? And even the women?
KAINJI: Don't worry. We'll take care of them.
ATLANTIC: How? What do you propose?
KAINJI (*Pensive.*) Hnm... Government is not blind or asleep, you know. We have secret agents. Constant armed surveillance. We use the police too to check.
ATLANTIC: So you know the trouble makers?
KAINJI: Precisely! No government should be taken for granted. We're keeping our records. The General orders that no stone be left unturned.
ATLANTIC: What precisely? What concrete plans?
KAINJI: Oh well, we have our secret agents right there with them in the market place.
ATLANTIC: Great!
KAINJI: We'll silence anybody who dares speak against, challenge or sabotage our government. We've dispatched our boys into all nooks and corners of the land. Even in the marketplace.
ATLANTIC: Ah, those rowdy traders!
(*The Chief approaches now but they are not aware.*)

KAINJI: Well, the bottom line is... I mean with all the sacrifices we're making, it's only fair that we pay ourselves first.
ATLANTIC (*Chuckling.*): Earn as you work.
KAINJI: Yeah! It's a deal.
ATLANTIC: Sounds reasonable to me.
KAINJI (*Playfully.*): Earn as you work.
ATLANTIC: Right! The best I've learnt so far! (*Warm hand-shakes.*)
KAINJI: Our share. It's a deal! (*Suddenly the Chief enters. They're startled.*)
CHIEF (*Laughing.*): And my share too!
ATLANTIC (*Stammering.*): Wha..wha... You...Your share?
KAINJI: What share?
CHIEF: I heard something about shares. (*OSHUN peeps from her corner but they don't see her.*) I too want mine. Yes. My share!
ATLANTIC: Oh no. Not now...Not now, my friend. Ehm...(*Coughs.*) You mis...mis-read...mis...heard.
CHIEF: Oh no.
KAINJI: Well, mis-spoke. (*Coughs.*) Ehm...Chief! (*Praising...*) Our great Chief! Lord of the land!
ATLANTIC (*Recovering.*) The Land Lord!
CHIEF: That's me! Yes my share. Whoever works has to get a share.
KAINJI: True, true. But you're wrong. You didn't hear right.
CHIEF: What? No shares?
KAINJI: Nothing. Nothing to share. At least not now.
ATLANTIC (*Recovering.*): Except the responsibilities.
CHIEF: Those too. But my ears heard right. You know the blind man says he's heard people talking about sharing. So unless the whole thing is divided again he's not going not accept it. (*They laugh.*)
KAINJI (*Teasing.*): Oh Chief. Funny man. Always asking for *your* share. Makes one think of you as a tax collector.
ATLANTIC: Are you, Chief? (*They all laugh. The Government Official rises.*) I must be going now. Time for the Cabinet Meeting.
CHIEF: Make sure you tell them about us. Represent our interest.
KAINJI: Always. Always.
ATLANTIC: (*A handshake with Government Official.*) Our interest. Remember?
KAINJI: My word! (*Exit Government. ATLANTIC walks back to the lounge. The Chief follows. They sit.*)
CHIEF (*Coughs.*): These Government Officials! Never trust them.
ATLANTIC: True? I've heard that a billion times.
CHIEF (*Whispering.*): I tell you, be careful.

ATLANTIC: But why precisely?
CHIEF: They're greedy. Oh so greedy! (*Coughs, adjusts his seat.*) Government workers working for themselves. Ha! Ha! Ha!
ATLANTIC (*Laughing.*): You all... I know. Ha!
CHIEF: That's why you must listen to me. (*Pause.*) You see that new place by my village where you just struck a new oil well? (*ATLANTIC is silently studying him.*) Well, the people there, too, are my own people.
ATLANTIC: Meaning?
CHIEF: Compensation.
ATLANTIC: Oh yes! We'll compensate the people as usual.
CHIEF: Yes. Pay. Through *me*.
ATLANTIC: How much?
CHIEF: You know, the usual thing.
ATLANTIC: But it's a very small well.
CHIEF (*Laughing.*): Yes, as they say, 'the swallow's smile can only be as big as his mouth'. Not so?
ATLANTIC: Hmmm...You people and your proverbs! Well, I guess...I do.
CHIEF: So make the payments in *my* name. I'm their leader, after all.
ATLANTIC: But Chief. You need to understand the way government works.
CHIEF: Oh, don't tell me that. I know. Remember I too was in government? Yes, a civil servant. I slaved... My friend, a government *slave*. That is what a civil servant means.
ATLANTIC: I hear you. But the rule with the Government is that all compensation should go to the community to ensure that everyone is paid. You know everyone in that village must be displaced to the camp...moved to the camp. Nothing there yet.
CHIEF: Oh, yes. They will get...I mean, through me. I'm their Chief, their leader. No one goes to the community...land...except through me. And no one comes to it or to you, except through me.
ATLANTIC (*Chuckling.*): The millennium messiah!
CHIEF: Sure! I am the way. The truth...
ATLANTIC: But not the life?
CHIEF: Oh, yes. I am. Everything!
ATLANTIC: Yeah, the deity. Ha! No one goes to heaven alive. (*They laugh.*) And so you got everyone coming and going. (*More laughter.*)
CHIEF: That's it!
ATLANTIC: And you must write your own ticket.
CHIEF: Yes. Here. Right here! (*He pushes a sheet of paper. ATLANTIC studies it. Alarmed.*)
ATLANTIC: Isn't this too much?

CHIEF: The cost of everything's going up, you know. Inflation.
ATLANTIC: That too I understand. But here the rate of inflation's higher than that of production. (*Chief is silent then resolves.*)
CHIEF: Ok. Pay a million then. Half for the community. The other half to me per-sonally. (*ATLANTIC stunned, silent.*) Yes, fair enough. That will do for the incidental costs. You never know. As we say, the farmer who goes to the farm must be armed with enough drinking water. You cannot cry without eyes. Can you?
ATLANTIC: I guess not. Hnm...Interesting... Ok you got a deal.
CHIEF: And one more deal to keep you smiling all the way to the bank.
ATLANTIC: Yes. Be quick.
CHIEF: I know. '*Deal's*' your other name.
ATLANTIC: No apologies. Isn't that what we're here for?
CHIEF: Ok. (*Coughs, clears his throat and draws near.*) In addition to my brother's daughter, OBIDA...
ATLANTIC: Who?
CHIEF: Our daughter that I gave to your European friend. (*Silence.*) Or you've forgotten?
ATLANTIC: Which? No. The American? Sure I remember! So what about her?
CHIEF: Nothing. Just to say she's fine...Yes... fine... and pleased...
ATLANTIC: Had to be. That guy...
CHIEF: A multi billionaire, I hear.
ATLANTIC: Great guy. He can the buy entire Third World. (*Drinks.*) That girl is lucky.
CHIEF: Very lucky. (*Pause, scratches his head.*) Hnm... and that is why I must give you another. One good turn deserves another. Isn't that what they say?
ATLANTIC: Oh, yes. (*Thinking.*) That other girl...I mean your daughter. How's she anyway? Do you hear from her?
CHIEF: Regularly. Tells me it's winter...deadly cold over there now.
ATLANTIC: That is true.
CHIEF: She's complains
ATLANTIC: Really?
CHIEF: Says she wants to come back. You know women. Like to...ehm...always complaining. What men have to bear! Ha!
ATLANTIC: OBIDA. "Fun girl she was," so my friend wrote. I'm surprised.
CHIEF: That is why I'm offering this other one...
ATLANTIC: What? Who?
CHIEF: A sweet daughter of the land. Take. Take her to Europe...I mean to

America for your next recess. I know how important it is for a hard working man to relax. Ha! What are friends for, afterall? You'll be blessed with this one.
ATLANTIC: Women ...
CHIEF: Evil.
ATLANTIC: Partners.
CHIEF: Necessary evil.
ATLANTIC: That's why you have so many?
CHIEF: What can we do? Man must wack! (*Chuckles.*) You'll be blessed with this one.
ATLANTIC: But Chief. You can see my hands are full. My wife's out there, you know. And now...
CHIEF: KOKO?
ATLANTIC: OSHUN.
CHIEF: No. KOKO. Her sister.
ATLANTIC: The hawker?
CHIEF: Got it!
ATLANTIC: Her?
CHIEF: Young. Juicy. Makes a man... (*Coughs.*) Jump...
ATLANTIC: I'm tired, man.
CHIEF: Goes with the territory. Women... (*Pause.*) Take her. Take her.
ATLANTIC: Hnm...Let me think.
CHIEF: Feel free to pass her on to any of your friends over there. All I ask in return is that you pass on your Landcruiser to me.
ATLANTIC: (*Stunned.*) What? My Landcruiser?
CHIEF: Yes. A very modest price for such a delicious offering...I mean gift...Most fertile land, my friend. Count your blessings.
ATLANTIC: As you like it. But what do you need this one for? You still have the other Range Rover you took for the other one...that OBIDA girl.
CHIEF: That was one deal. This is another. Not so?
ATLANTIC: I guess. (*Pause.*) So when is she coming?
CHIEF: Name your day.
ATLANTIC: Anytime soon?
CHIEF: At your pleasure!
ATLANTIC: If you insist.
CHIEF: I do. The *Landlord*, remember?
ATLANTIC: Sure always. (*They shake hands. Exit Chief. He ruminates. Alone. Shortly after his departure, OSHUN draped with the white sheet from the lounge table crawls out of hiding and hastens to the market-square. Then lights pick up the Chief who's now alone on his*

*way home from the GRA Oil Club. He appears to be troubled.*)

CHIEF (*Alone.*) OBIDA? Yes. That deaf daughter. 'Eneke nti mkpo'. Deaf! Deaf like that Eneke bird. Since she left for Europe, I haven't heard from that girl. Not even a word to say, 'Here, uncle. Take this dollar or pound sterling to buy yourself some tobacco, snuff, soap or oil to grease your chapped...' Oh, these children! Except just for a few who do remember that you labored for them. A lot of children are so ungrateful. So self-centered. Always taking and taking and expecting parents to do even more and more. (*Deep sigh.*) What loss parents suffer? You labor, hope to gain out of your own investment. But all you get back is nothing. Nothing! (*Fuming, his pace quickens now.*) I'm going to write to that senseless girl. Tell her what her mates abroad are doing at home, especially in the cities. Mansions here. Mansions there. Expensive estates springing up like mushrooms everywhere. Been to the banks lately? A new spectacle. No room to breathe. The once wretched mothers and fathers now choke the air as they'd line up to collect the thousands and thousands of foreign money sent to them by their children abroad. But not my own. No, not mine. Stupid girl! She's forgotten me. Drinking tea, milk and all the juices from those white men. Ha! (*Spits.*) Shame! Shame on you, OBIDA! You who go to the white-man's land to forget your very own. This is the day. I must...must write and tell her my mind. Do something now or never. Ungrateful child. After all I've done for her since they killed her father? And then her mother? That Jesse oil hell fire? The struggle for oil? Take...taken...so many. Aaaah...(*Pause.*) And I just wanted to help. Help her from the hell....Now what has she given to pay me back? Nothing. Nothing but disgrace...pain...Ah! That girl will pay back...And if not, she'll cease to be mine...mine...Not even in death for I will disown her. Thank God she's only a girl. Could you imagine her as a son to whom I'd have to bestow my own line...legacy? No way! (*Pause, smiles*) This other daughter...KOKO, I mean, is the answer to line my empty pockets. Yes. I need another car. Yes! I'm selling...God I'm 'sending' her with him...the white man. That crafty man who has so much but still counts every penny he gives or pays for anything. God! They're so stingy, these foreigners! Well, I too will get...my share...*My* share! And that's it. All I want. To make it up... (*His face suddenly lights up.*) Aaah, KOKO! KOKO, honey-sweet as freshly brewed wine in the morning dew (*Smacking his lips.*) Nice. Juicy like the succulent fruits she sells. Oh, such a great diet! And as I grabbed her fruit? Split open? And bit into that succulent pulp? Ha! She struggled, struggled and cried out loud to be saved. Saved? From what, Baptism? Indeed, that's all it was. A Baptism. For I could tell from the thick and narrow walls inside that the fruit was still green. Until I bit into it. Chaam! Ha! (*He quickens his pace towards his home as OSHUN crosses to the other side of the market-square.*)

OSHUN (*Frantic.*) I'm going to tell...Mother...OBIDA... KAINJI? Ah! I'll take him now to that place. Teach them a lesson. Let the war begin! Now! Now's the time to do it. And my sister, KOKO? My God, where's she? Where? Just hope she's not returning to sell in that place. No! (*Running.*) Sister, I'm with you. Now! All the way. You'll never be alone again. Never! I'll be with you till the very end. Oh, God, I'm coming! I'm going. Now! (*Running. The lights escort her into the next stage.*)

# MOVEMENT SIX

(*OSHUN returns to the GRA/Oil Club, where ATLANTIC and The Government Official are meeting. They are signing some documents but as soon as they see her coming, they quickly dash into the room with the files. OSHUN waits outside, humming a somber tune until the men return and let her in. Just then, two young men (one of them is OSHUN's lover wearing a mask) try to open the iron gate. But they can't. They bow and plead several times, hoping that ATLANTIC and the Government Official would let them in but they simply give them a nasty glare until the disgusted ATLANTIC rises and blows his whistle. Immediately his guard storms the scene from behind, salutes his master and awaits his orders.*)

ATLANTIC: Arrest those robbers!
GUARD: Yes saar!
ATLANTIC: Teach them a hard lesson.
GUARD: Yes saar! (*The guard makes a quick dash for the youths. The one arrested is OSHUN's lover, while the other flees with a scream: "See you tomorrow!" The arrested youth pleads frantically for freedom and mercy. "I no do anytin. I no be tief. I no fuck him wife. Na only job I want. Na only food. Just food I dey find. I beg. I beg, broda, help me. Help me beg am. Beg Oyiboman for me. Na beg I dey beg!" His pleading and protestations continue as the youth is dragged through the door behind, followed with a loud noise. The Government Official departs hurriedly. ATLANTIC leans back again to light a cigar. He reaches out for the radio, tunes into a slow jam music station as he continues to smoke and pace up and down in his deep thought.*)
ATLANTIC (*To OSHUN.*) Come now, sugar! (*OSHUN is silent but agitated.*)
ATLANTIC (*Puffing away smoke.*) Do come now. What was he saying?
OSHUN: You mean *crying*?
ATLANTIC: Same to me...Their crying and talking. They blame me for...
OSHUN: Nothing. Just nothing. You are beyond blame. It's just us. We are the problem.
ATLANTIC (*Studying her.*): True. Baby, you're so honest, so different from everyone else. (*Pause. Smokes.*) Only sometimes I can't... don't understand...I mean especially with that young man. Afterall, they're your people.
OSHUN: I know (*Reassuring smiles.*) No problem. It's not me you should fear.

ATLANTIC: But whom?
OSHUN: Nobody. Afterall, are you no longer in control?
ATLANTIC: Certainly.
OSHUN: So why fear...?
ATLANTIC (*Thinking.*): Control? (*Pause.*) But these people...
OSHUN: I know.
ATLANTIC: Don't trust... I mean soon, you too might be telling me he's your brother. And that one is your uncle. (*Chuckling.*) You black women and your imagnary brothers and uncles! Ha! (*They're interrupted by the wailing of the youth inside the cell. Outside, sounds of protests are also rising and drawing nearer. OSHUN fights her anxiety and rage. ATLANTIC is trying to pull her to his bosom, but she resists.*)
OSHUN: Oga, please release me. Let me go. (*She hums a tune: "Please release me."*)
ATLANTIC: I have you. Where do you think you're going?
OSHUN: Home.
ATLANTIC: Where? (*Loud laughter.*)
OSHUN: My place.
ATLANTIC: Where's that? (*Laughs.*) Don't be ridiculous. You belong here...in my arms.
OSHUN: To rule?
ATLANTIC: Damn the rules! All I want is my own...
OSHUN (*Cursing in her language.*): *Death*! No. Quick, o'jare! Let me go? Stop wasting my bloody time.
ATLANTIC: What? (*Silence.*) What did you say?
OSHUN: Nothing...Yet. (*Explodes into laughter.*)
ATLANTIC: You silly girl. Why be in such a rush?
OSHUN (*Reading her watch.*): It's time. Time. I'm done.
ATLANTIC (*Angry*): With me?
OSHUN: Oh, come on. Don't take it personally. Time respects no king or master. I have to go. My people...
ATLANTIC: Your people?
OSHUN (*Laughing.*) Who else? It's been so long. My mother is waiting. I have to go...
ATLANTIC: Join them.
OSHUN: (*Laughs, plays with his chin.*) To get paid!
ATLANTIC: Not now. You have to wait.
OSHUN: Till when? How long?
ATLANTIC: But tell me, why are you in such a hurry now?
OSHUN (*More agitated.*): But I've been here, waiting all this time. I'm tired.

See you. (*Picks up her shoes.*)
ATLANTIC: Why are you acting up? You crazy?
OSHUN (*Snapping.*): To you. Just pay me.
ATLANTIC: Money. That's all?
OSHUN: Yes! A worker expects to be paid. Is that too much to ask the director?
ATLANTIC: May be not. But...(*Checks himself.*) You're not...not just a worker. And after all these special moments? Don't you think you mean more...I mean more than a worker? Babe, you need to think better of yourself.
OSHUN: Does that put money into my pocket? Feed me? Pay the bills?
ATLANTIC: Hey, wait a minute. This talk about money-money-money! Pay-pay-pay! Is that all there is to it? All that you people think about?
OSHUN: That's all. What else do hungry people think about?
ATLANTIC: But Babe, you're not like them. You're different. (*Silence.*) So different. Why this sudden change?
OSHUN: Your teaching, maybe?
ATLANTIC: But haven't I been treating...taking care of you?
OSHUN: That you have. But don't you think I can do it better for myself? Instead of having to depend...(*Pause.*) Anyway, I'm on my way now. Got to move on! (*She picks up her bag.*)
ATLANTIC: Babe, I don't understand you anymore. What are you trying to say?
OSHUN: Precisely what I just said. I'm ready. On my way now.
ATLANTIC: You may. It's your choice. I can't help...give you anything now.
OSHUN: So when?
ATLANTIC: Not until you behave...know yourself.
OSHUN: I see. (*Tersely.*) ATLANTIC, I need my money and I need to go. Now! (*Silence as they stand staring at each other.*)
ATLANTIC: Do as you please.
OSHUN (*Smiling, walking away.*): Ok, I'll be back.
ATLANTIC (*Pulling her back.*): Silly girl! One of those your mood swings again? You know I just how I feel about...Oh, well, tell me you're not leaving.
OSHUN (*Smiling.*): I said it already. I *will* be back.
ATLANTIC: I will be waiting here, Babe. And tell me you won't be long.
OSHUN (*Hesitates, smiles.*): Ok. I won't. (*Spotlights following her. She steadily walks away without looking back. ATLANTIC escorts her with his lustful eyes. Once she's gone, he slumps into he lounge chair, lights a cigarette and starts puffing away smoke. Alone.*)
ATLANTIC (*Sighs*): She's been acting up lately. Hnm... Who knows? Who

knows what's eating her up? So young? I thought I'd find peace with this one. They're usually better young, juicy, easier to manage. At least before they grow into that premenopausal phase. Ha! The moon phase I call it! I know it, I can see it coming. Yes, I saw it in my first wife, Judy. Then Katie. And now this one? But she's too young...Oh, well, women...never too young to give a man heartaches. I've had it with them. Whatever you do as a man. You can never please them. Strange. Strange. Women! And this breed here? Even stranger. (*The gate cracks open. In a swift movement, OSHUN crosses behind. Startled, not exactly sure of what he saw, ATLANTIC walks to the iron gate to check and reinforce the lock. Meanwhile, OSHUN goes behind to release her lover, the Guard. But for the birds chirping, and his dog's barking, everything appears calm as he returns, pours himself a drink and continues musing.*) Actually reminds me of my wife at home. Who knows what she's doing now? Been acting up even more lately. Must be having her usual shopping spree. Katie..."Born to Shop." That should have been her name. (*Parodying her.*) "Oh, darling! Just this one more diamond. I want it. Now. Just this." What can you do but be a man...and yield? To her, yes. But not this one. (*Chuckles.*) Cute... My Cutie! I just love her...Much like the child I should have...but never had. (*Pause.*) I wish... Well, too late now. Maybe it's the reason I want her so...So bad. Does she...Does she really know that I care? Well, what does it matter? She's just another country girl. We've been warned. Told not give these natives, especially their girls the impression that we have money and yield to their demands. They'll get spoilt. Start expecting too much. And when you stop? Ha! Sour grapes! No. Can't risk that. A woman's wrath? Beware, man. Beware! If you come out of it alive. You'll never be the same. Scalded. For life. Been there, done that! So this one too expects me to yield to blackmail? No way. I won't...Let a woman take advantage of me? No! No more! (*Pause.*) But I've got to keep on playing. (*Looks at his watch.*) My God, how time flies! Soon I'll be gone. Write her, Katie? My wife...My life...(*Another look at his watch. Sits and starts writing when suddenly, OSHUN storms back into the scene to confront ATLANTIC. He jumps, screams, "My Gaaad!"*)

OSHUN (*In his face.*) Here! My time. Get ready!
ATLANTIC: I'll be damned! How did you get in here?
OSHUN: Don't ask. Just pay. Pay me.
ATLANTIC: What's come over you? You crazy?

OSHUN: Right. Pay me.

ATLANTIC: I see. (*Silence as ATLANTIC stands gazing at her, until he explodes.*) You too? Ungrateful b...! Harassing me after all I've given...done for you?

OSHUN: You've done nothing. Given nothing.

ATLANTIC (*Mock laughter.*): Really?

OSHUN: Yes!

ATLANTIC: Ok. My gold watch? Give it back.

OSHUN (*Flinging it.*): That's it. Take. As if I that's important. Ha! Ha! Ha! You think I care? I don't!

ATLANTIC: (*Stunned.*) I can't believe this. OSHUN? You? You too? well, I'll be danmed! (*Sighs.*) I thought you were...were not like these people. (*Silence.*) But...but tell me...What...what...What is it you want?

OSHUN: What you owe.

ATLANTIC (*Exploding.*) Dammit! I owe you nothing. Nothing!

OSHUN: Really? You'll soon find out.

ATLANTIC (*Furious.*): Out! (*OSHUN is smiling but defiant.*) You get on my nerves! You're just like them. Another piece of trash. Get out of here. Now!

OSHUN: Don't you touch me!

ATLANTIC: What? Who are you?

OSHUN (*Calmly.*): You'll soon find out.

ATLANTIC: What nonsense! (*He steps forward to push her.*)

OSHUN: Try! Just dare to touch me. And you'll be sorry for it...Everything!

ATLANTIC (*Shocked.*) So this is it? (*Pause.*) But I don't blame you. It's me...my mistake. I trusted... invested in...in...nothing. (*Reflecting.*) And all I got is suckers. Suckers!

OSHUN (*Mock laughter.*): Like you, sir. You taught us well.

ATLANTIC: Go-da-mmit! I paid for it...for everything! Nonsense! You people suck. Nothing but suckers. Never to render any service with... without inflating...satisfaction.

OSHUN: Is it by force?

ATLANTIC: What the hell am I doing with this fuc...illiterate...?

OSHUN (*Smiling.*): I've seen your betters.

ATLANTIC: And you think I haven't? Ha! This nation of crooks and bastards!

OSHUN (*In his face.*): You people. All you want is to get something out of nothing. Not so?

ATLANTIC: What? Look who's talking. The sucker herself! I paid my dues... fully.

OSHUN: To whom? No, you haven't. You owe your life to us... this very land.

ATLANTIC: You land of liars! Stinking debtor-nation. Aren't you ashamed? All potentials and morality sold. Auctioned to the highest bidder. Out of my sight! Bitch!
OSHUN (*Strutting.*): Call me what you like. But beware.
ATLANTIC: Me?
OSHUN (*Emphatically.*): Yes, you *be-ware*. You can't take me or anyone here for a ride anymore. No. No more jolly rides, you white master!
ATLANTIC: That's easy. You'll see!
OSHUN: Dare! (*She sits on the lounge chair and dares him to push her out. Behind them, the Guard/Lover escapes with ATLANTIC's gun, the imprisoned youth following him behind.*)
ATLANTIC: You get on my nerves. Get out! Out of my sight! You're trespassing on my property!
OSHUN: Tres-passing? On *my* land! Ha! Albino. You are joking! (*ATLANTIC is so enraged, he runs in to fetch his gun.*)
ATLANTIC: Just wait. We'll know who rules... (*Tries to push her out.*)
OSHUN: Don't you dare touch me!
ATLANTIC (*Advancing threateningly.*): I will. (*Smokes.*) But you're only a woman. I'll have to restrain myself...Restraint, a scarce commodity in this savage land. Yes!
OSHUN (*Defiantly.*): Your concern? Just try me! Ha! Ha! Ha!
ATLANTIC: What for? You worthless...
OSHUN (*Hysterical laughter.*): Ha! Ha! Ha! We'll see.
ATLANTIC: Are you threatening me? Remember whom you are talking to? I'm the Director of Sh...
OSHUN (*Saluting.*): Shame! Precisely.
ATLANTIC: You'll be sorry for this. All of you.
OSHUN: Sorry for what?
ATLANTIC (*Dials the phone.*): I'm calling Headquarters for security rein-force-ment. Get ready.
OSHUN: And who says we're not?
ATLANTIC: Ok. We'll see who wins this war.
OSHUN (*Mock laughter.*) We'll see!
OSHUN: We are the bastards, remember? My friend, pay. Pay up your debts.
ATLANTIC: Who's your friend?
OSHUN: Ok, my enemy then. Better still. Pay up.
ATLANTIC: I don't owe you a thing, you worthless pros...
OSHUN: I'm worthless to you now because I want my rights?
ATLANTIC: Your...? Nonsense! I'm giving nothing. If you don't like my decision, then too bad. Or better still, go to court. I'm ready.

OSHUN: Really? Then get ready. (*She explodes into laughter. Stops suddenly, and confronts him.*)
OSHUN: Like you too, master, I fix my price for my buyers. Don't you fix the price for the goods you sell to us? Do we dictate the price for you to sell? So why should it be different for us? You come to our own land. You take and take and also dictate the price? And still we have no rights to say 'no'? Haba, Monsieur le Directeur! Where is your avowed justice? Where is your fairness? A deal is a deal.
ATLANTIC: A deal? With whom?
OSHUN: With you, man!
ATLANTIC: Ridiculous.
OSHUN: To you, I fix my price: $5? $10? And all night long, everything adds up. (*Vulgar display of her body. ATLANTIC is now completely disgusted and moves away as he smokes and observes her with scorn.*) You touch? $10. Suck? A double blow. And then the big one? Ah, Mr. Director? You think you can just continue to pour and discharge all that for nothing? And then Aids? Add that too. Ah, Oga, Director! What if? What if? And then the other risk? Unwanted baby. My dear, will...Will you raise the baby? *Our* baby? No, you won't. All you want is just to kick us around and out...to clean up your mess... To drain...To drill... No, man. Not any more! You pour it? You pay for it! You pump it? You pay for it. You mess it up? *You* clean it up! (*Silence as the incredulous ATLANTIC smokes and observes from a corner while she takes centre-stage.*)
OSHUN: Or what do you think I am? A piece of stone?
ATLANTIC (*Rises, grabs the phone.*): Shit! Can't take it anymore.
OSHUN: You wanted it. Brought me here. Paid me pennies all day and you want to kiss? Pay up man. All day long you took my bra. My panties, you put under your pillow and you've been sniffing and sniffing and touching and sucking...And then you poured all that into...God! Don't you know it costs money? You think I'm worth nothing? Well, I tell you now Oyibo, you've taken and taken. It's about time. Now. Pay up. We don't run charities here. Isn't that what you say? Well, hear. I'm no Charity. My name is OSHUN. Nothing goes for nothing. That's what you taught us. You know what that means? I know you don't. Better go find out because I'm not just a mere local chicken that you pluck out her plumes and throw into your bowl of soup to eat just like that. Oh, no. You *can't*, continue to eat me for nothing, you Director of Shame! You've sucked and drained enough. Now pay up, man!

ATLANTIC: You're just a slut. That's all. I picked you up. Remember?

OSHUN: And is that why you must devalue...I mean make me lose my entire worth and self-respect? Ah, man. Even a prostitute, too, has her dignity and humanity.

ATLANTIC: Look who's talking! Did you ever have any?

OSHUN (*Takes out a scroll of paper from her bag.*) Look. I have my degree.

ATLANTIC (*Startled, jumps.*): A what?

OSHUN: I said *diplomas*!

ATLANTIC: What? You kidding! Can't...can't be right.

(*He sits back, contemplating this new development.*)

OSHUN: Well, I am. I didn't speak with water in my mouth, did I? (*Lifting the papers like some sacred testament.*) Yes, certificates. Not one, but two. Worked my butt off to earn them both. (*Deep sigh.*) Like you too, I have them. Earned them. And many others like me in this land...with a load of degrees! But see? Where are we now? Where? You have the upper hand because your country lifts you up. And mine abandons, forsakes, betrays me...all of us... with you in control...

ATLANTIC: So... so...?

OSHUN: God decrees fairness! Look, whiteman. If not for this condition we're in? No jobs...no amenities...no rights... (*Sighs.*) Just this permanent condition of joblessness. Ah! You think I'll be here hawking my precious body to earn a living? And you, squeezing and taking undue advantage of me...of us...and everything? Just what do you think you are?

ATLANTIC: (*Smiling, smoking.*) The Director. (*Crosses his legs.*) The one and only authority in charge here. Hey, won't you thank me for my sacrifices? Risking my precious life to make...manage your resources? This bloody country without a leader? Don't you ever blame me. I take what I can get. Afterall, your so-called leaders gave me the power.

OSHUN: No. Only the contracts!

ATLANTIC (*Laughing.*) What's the difference between contracts and power? (*OSHUN stares at him spitefully.*) Woman, tell me. What is? Ha! Ha! Ha! Better know it. Interests rule the world.

OSHUN: Self interest...

ATLANTIC: Right! Don't you think I too have a right to seek mine? Protect my own interests?

OSHUN: At whose expense? Mine? Our land? The impoverished women and youths?

ATLANTIC: Does it matter? And who cares?

OSHUN: Oh hear him! (*Parodying*) Ha! "Does it matter?" No it *doesn't*! So let's exchange positions; you take mine. I take yours. Exchange is no robbery. Isn't that what they say?

ATLANTIC (*Laughing*): Woman, I can see that you are suffering from an acute strain of Idealism. An acute deficiency of Realism, rather. And I sympathize with you. But be advised. In today's world, one thing sells fast; Capitalism, forged on individual, private interest, seasoned by national...No my dear. Idealism...communal...well, communism...a ready formula for loss, perpetual want, denials, and bankruptcy. It just can't, and won't sell. A very High Risk venture capital that just won't sell in our wired world today.

OSHUN: Hence you bind us, hands and feet?

ATLANTIC: No. Tell you what. Try the emerging global market. To succeed? Profit. Profit. Profit. The new creed of success. That's the new Reality. Trust me. It sells. And sells at high costs in today's stock market. Young woman, look at it this way. You can't take your hopes, and Idealism to the bank. Can you? But Reality. The real stock...?

OSHUN: Hello! You just proved my point. Reality is me. Now. So pay me. I'm ready to go to the bank!

ATLANTIC (*Smiling.*): But woman. Don't you know I am the bank you have to go to? I am the director, remember?

OSHUN: Whose? Not mine. (*ATLANTIC finally loses his temper and yells "Out!" He pushes her. OSHUN falls, rises and confronts him as he struggles to overcome her.*)

ATLANTIC: Guard! Guard! Come and get this sucker out of here. (*No response. The struggle continues.*) That fool. Where is he now?

OSHUN: Are you asking me?

ATLANTIC: He's your bloody countryman. Is he not? You planned this. A set up. (*ATLANTIC tries to reach to the closet to pull out his gun, but OSHUN shouts something to the Guard in their local language.*).

ATLANTIC: Shut up!

OSHUN: No you can't. I'm through. Not in my land! Our land! Oyibo. You are a visitor. A guest must not be allowed to sit on top of the owners of the land, suffocate them and then take away the seat with him as he leaves...

ATLANTIC (*Frustrated.*): Guard! Guard! (*Silence.*) That guard? He's fired! Fired! That idiot? Fired! He'll never work for me any more. Gooooolie! These people. Can't trust them.

OSHUN: And you? Can we trust you? Hey! Makes us equal. You taught us well. (*With both of them locked in each other's arms, the militant*

*chants grow urgent, nearer. ATLANTIC listens, terror-stricken. His arms fall, limp. OSHUN is now free.)*
ATLANTIC (*Alarmed.*) You...you...gang...set up...Is it?
OSHUN: My time! (*She bursts into laughter as her lover, the guard storms the gate with the mob in a non-violent protest. They're clamoring, banging at the locked gate. ATLANTIC stands stupefied, frozen; his hands fall limp. OSHUN hurries to join the mob as they cheer, jeer and mock at ATLANTIC with some women dressed like him in tie and shirt. He recovers, briefly, then grabs the phone to call the Government Official. Blackout.)*

# MOVEMENT SEVEN

(*Same location at the GRA/OIL Club. ATLANTIC, the Chief and the Government Official are in conference. The people's drumbeats keep throbbing in the background. ATLANTIC is worried and exasperated.*)

KAINJI: This is getting out of hand.
ETHIOPE: Something, something's got to be done.
ATLANTIC: Absolutely important. Safety! Safety of our precious lives and interests.
ETHIOPE & KAINJI: We know.
ATLANTIC (*To KAINJI.*): As the appointed national authority on petroleum...
KAINJI: I know...
ATLANTIC: Our deal. Remember?
KAINJI (*Patting his back.*): Trust, man.
ATLANTIC: I'm trying. But...
KAINJI (*Fist salute.*): We're bound...
ETHIOPE & ATLANTIC (*With fist salutes.*): Together!
ATLANTIC (*To ETHIOPE*) I will always do my best. (*Pause.*) And Chief, you too...
ETHIOPE: Sure-sure!
KAINJI: Let's try this. Hire more guards.
ATLANTIC: And Chief, be sure to tell those natives what the consequences of these riots will be. It's your responsibility. Ensure that your people are brought under control. Be firm. Tell them that violence will cost them even more than they're asking for now. We can't tolerate any irresponsible acts. Chief, control. Control your people. It's your part to play. And we'll depend...(*A loud explosion drowns his voice. ATLANTIC rises quickly, goes to fetch a bill board where he writes: "Wanted: ONE GUARD. Qualifications: HONEST, DEPENDABLE, STRONG, HARDWORKING, MUST SPEAK ENGLISH." Trailed by the men, ATLANTIC now goes to mount the advertisement high up at the gate. Another loud explosion. Then they see the mob running to them from various directions. ATLANTIC quickly shuts the gate and they return to their meeting.*)
ATLANTIC: See? See what I'm saying?
KAINJI: Who knows where they're going?
ATLANTIC But you saw them coming.
ETHIOPE (*Nudging.*): KAINJI, better go and see.

KAINJI: But you're their Chief...
ATLANTIC: Yes, Chief. Go meet them.
ETHIOPE: Why me?
ATLANTIC: They're your people.
KAINJI: They'll listen to you better.
ETHIOPE: These women and youths to listen? To whom?
ATLANTIC & KAINJI: You, their beloved Chief.
ETHIOPE: You must be joking. Or you simply are blind to their nature. Even the blind and deaf can tell that the voices you hear out there, today's women and youths are no longer what they used to be.
ATLANTIC & KAINJI: How?
ETHIOPE (*Emphatically.*): They don't...won't listen to us...anyone...Not anymore.
ATLANTIC: Then get ready. They must be taught to listen. Order! Order! The rule of the law. Somebody has to be in control here. And that authority is you, Chief.
ETHIOPE: Me? But you're the Director.
ATLANTIC: Oh no. Cut it out. The Government Official and I...We're both strangers in this land.
ETHIOPE: But he's the appointed Government Official.
ATLANTIC: Yes, from the North.
KAINJI: And you from the West.
ETHIOPE: So what are you both doing here?
KAINJI & ATLANTIC: Interests...Others...ours...
ETHIOPE (*Indicating KAINJI.*) ATLANTIC, yours I can understand. But KAINJI, you and I are both citizens of this country. We share...
(*Another loud explosion.*)
KAINJI (*Impatiently.*) I know. So what do you want me to do now? Time is not on our side anymore. Tell me.
ATLANTIC: First thing first. Tell them. Stop them.
ETHIOPE (*Rising.*) Teach them. Teach them to listen.
ETHIOPE: We will.
KAINJI (*Irritated.*): We must!
ATLANTIC (*Handing KAINJI the poster bill to mount.*): Control! Control! Control!
ETHIOPE: We'll keep on trying. (*Silence. KAINJI starts to mount the poster-ad. ATLANTIC tries to refill his pipe, but it's empty. He goes into the room behind to fetch his needs. Rowdy chants, with loud explosions tear through the smoky humid air. The mob now swells around the locked gate. Seeing them, the Chief quickly disappears through the*

*nearest exit. Too late; KAINJI can neither go forward nor backward. So he retreats to join ATLANTIC at the door, where they stand watching this developing battle-ground. Armed with the placards and certificates, the jobless come head-on, rushing, pushing and surging forward for vantage positions at the gate.)*

ATLANTIC: My Gaaaaad! Look. The whole damned country is at the gate. Waiting. Waiting for handouts! (*Sighs.*)

KAINJI: But it's only one job.

ATLANTIC: Just one vacancy for a guard. And they're all here? The whole nation? One hundred and twenty million of them? Goooolie! These people make me sick. Sick. Sick and tired of this stinking fuc... (*Screaming..*) Out! (*They ignore him and instead break into supplicating chants. "Help saar. We beg. Oga, I beg! Na beg we beg!"*)

ATLANTIC: Go away! Read the sign. One. Only one vacancy. I can't help you. (*KAINJI too adds his own threats.*)

KAINJI: Go away. The national security guards are coming!

MOB: Let them come. Let them come.

MOB LEADER: Today na today-o! We dey wait.

MOB CHORUS (*Stomping, drumming with anything within their reach.*): Wait! Wait! We go wait!

MOB CHORUS: We must enter! Enter! Enter! Enter!

ATLANTIC: We need guards. Guards! Security! Guards! (*As the people chant, they ram into the gate with their bodies, hoping to force it open. The phone in the corner rings. ATLANTIC rushes to answer. Stunned and terrified by the news he's just heard, he drops the phone.*)

ATLANTIC (*Alarmed.*) Gun shots?

KAINJI: Who?

ATLANTIC (*Shivering.*) My colleague.

KAINJI: Mob...Texac, off-shore.

ATLANTIC: Just narrowly escaped.

KAINJI: Again? My God! (*ATLANTIC nods.*)

ATLANTIC: The President General has summoned us to an emergency meeting.

KAINJI: Where? When?

ATLANTIC: At the headquarters. Tonight.

KAINJI: Then I must go right away.

ATLANTIC: After recruiting another guard from this horde. (*His voice is drowned by the chanting mob. "Get in line, everybody! One single file. They're coming! The Oga dey come! Yes, E dey come. I see-am! De white oga dey come. And de Government Official follow-am for back. See! See dem! And they carry gun too! Dem carry koboko," some shout. Others cry out "Bulala! Dem carry bulala!" Panic, pandemonium ensues. Not ready for this commotion, ATLANTIC pulls KAINJI from behind. They retreat inside to confer. Meanwhile, the mob continues their pleading and chattering outside. OSHUN, now masked, has joined the mob. Some of the frightened voices cry out? "So wetin? Wetin we fit do now?" Another voice responds to the question: 'No? Who dey (h)ask dat kind foolish question? Wetin we fit do now? Nonsense! Dat no be de question for we now? We get choice. De time to do sometin is now. No choice-No choice. We fit... fit do sometin. No matter how small. We fit do sometin." Another replies: "So wetin be dat small sometin we fit do? "Yes, dat na de question. Dat is it! Wetin we go do, Now? Wetin be dat small tin we go do now? E beta make we move forward and stop fighting each other. De bigger fight dey come, self. And if we no strong and fight together? We all go lose. Saaam-saam!" Then others take up the refrain.. "Na true. Yes. Na true talk be dat-o! Una hear! Dem get power pass us plenty-plenty: Na true-o! Na true-o. Dem don land-o! Make we move now! Make we act now!" Then a screaming voice intervenes: "Dem go beat sense out of we-o! Run! Commot! Make we run!" They panic and struggle for space as each one tries to push and edge out the other. As the shoving and struggling continues, the one who had raised the alarm, suddenly burst out laughing. "See them! See them! Fools! My people dey foolish proper-proper! Na (h)only yourself you sabi fight. Now shey una sabi fight? Fight de oga now? Where your power dey? Abi na (h)only to knock una teet and head commot una sabi? Get ready now. Oga dey come. Make una go knock dem teet and head commot too!" Briefly, he breaks into mock laughter and then starts to sing a familiar tune as the others watch in amusement.)*

MAN: They want a guard, not a nurse.
ANOTHER MAN : They want a guard...a security guard.
MAN: And that's a man's job.
WOMAN: Guard? Who says a woman can't do that job?
WOMEN: Who says? Who says? Just try us! Dare to try us!
WOMAN: What a man can do?
WOMEN: A woman can do...
WOMAN: Better!
WOMEN: Better! Better! Better! Women are better! (*Chanting, dancing.*)
    Women are better! Better! Better! Women are better!
MEN (*Shoving them aside.*) You women, give us a chance and go away.

MAN: Or better, go find your place in the kitchen. (*The men laugh*).
WOMAN: So you're men for nothing?
WOMEN: (*Teasing.*) Our good for nothing...
MEN: Shut up! Useless women!
WOMEN: Ohoo! They like to shut us up. Go and shut the oil wells!
WOMEN: Yes, the flaming oil well!
WOMEN: Dripping with our blood. Yes, shut them down! Shut down the Oil Club!
WOMAN: And dat yeye government?
WOMEN: Stop! Stop! Stop the bloody government!
WOMAN: With your so-called power, what can you do to the whiteman?
ANOTHER WOMAN: And the Government Official?
WOMEN: Go fight them now. Fight the Oil Club! Fight! Fight them! Fight them who are against us!
WOMAN (*Perhaps OBIDA, pushing her way through.*) Nonsense! You men should go roast in the oil fire. Yes, go fry your souls in the kitchen. Ok? (*The men are protesting and trying to shout her down but she's defiant.*) Don't you have hands to cook?
MAN: You women of nowadays with your long tails.
ANOTHER MAN: Only that? Long beaks!
MAN: To suck blood! Woman sabi make plenty-plenty blood.
WOMAN (*Protesting.*) And you eat them?
MAN: Blood or women?
ANOTHER MAN: Both. What's the difference? Woman is blood. Ha! Ha! Ha!
WOMAN: (*OBIDA.*): All that some of you men need is a good sharp knife to cut off   those long tail of yours.
WOMAN (*Laughing.*) That should keep them quite. Cut them to size.
WOMAN: At least for a while until they come crawling on their hands.
WOMAN: Den you chop am saam-saam like rotten yam...
WOMAN: To be cast off.
WOMEN: Fit only for the garbage! Ha! Ha! Ha!
MAN: You hear them?
MAN: Bloody women!
VOICE TWO: You too. Yeye men! That's how you people oppress us in this land just because we're...
VOICE: (Loud from behind.) Stop dis nonsense man-woman palava you all. Wetin? We dey cry here for beta tin. For we life and you just dey run your mouth like broken water pipe dey wet each other wey you all suppose to dey talk for each other. Abi? You know wetin life be? You scratch my back...

CHORUS: I scratch yours.
VOICE: Na soooo!
CHORUS: True-true!
VOICE TWO: But that doesn't mean we won't fight for ourselves, each of us.
CHORUS: Of course. No be why we come here?
VOICE TWO: Yes! That's why we poor people, man or woman, must join hands together to fight our common enemies, these rich and powerful people.
VOICE: Haba! So make una forget wetin dey between una, man-woman and begin to dey work together for all una beta.
CHORUS: Na true talk be dat!
VOICE ONE: Dat no be de case. Na de problem with this country. Everybody comes last and wants to be treated first! Shame! Shame on you all! (*Spits in disgust.*)
VOICE TWO: You know how long I've been waiting for this opportunity? (*Counting.*) One, two three, four, five, six. Six whole months of my life, just waiting to get this opportunity to be interviewed. And for what? Security Guard. Yes! With a university degree.
VOICE: That's all? Six months? My friend, you just got started.
VOICE: Keep quiet, my friend! You know how long I've been waiting myself?
ANGRY VOICES (*Shouting.*): So, who cares? Are we not all waiting too? Are we not all in the same sinking boat?
VOICE TWO (*As OSHUN?*): No, my people. Some of us have paddled their canoes ashore long before and ahead of others. Yes, some of us have long been in the sea, casting our nets wide, burning the midnight oil... with strong faith to catch fish. And actually with a lot of struggle. We did. We thought we were loaded. (*Dips into his pocket, wields degrees.*) These! These are the fishes I caught. But can I eat them? No? I caught fishes that are not edible. They've been here, right in my net. But I can neither eat nor sell them because nobody will buy my fish. Dead. Dead. My fishes are dead. And I'm still carrying them around. Just looking...looking for a buyer... My people, what does one do with a dead fish? It stinks? Throw it back into the sea? What then will I hold onto? What if the condition improves? The tide rises high and my fish comes back alive again? But then, my net is torn, I know. What if I can't catch any more...? What if? What if? My people. These are my questions to you all. Help me find answers. Pleeeeeassseee! (*She places her degrees at the center of the circle. Other frustrated youths join in this ritual act. Soon, they pile them up into a heap, ready to make a bonfire.*)

OTHER YOUNG VOICE: And you think you're alone? Here's mine.
ANOTHER VOICE: And mine!
ANOTHER VOICE: Mine too.
MORE VOICES: Mine! Mine! Mine! Mine tooooooo!
A VOICE: What do we do with trophies without meaning?
CHORUS: What? What do we do-what we do?
A VOICE (*Trying to light a march.*) Useless. They're useless.
ANOTHER VOICE: Our education is useless. Worthless!
A VOICE: So what do we do?
A VOICE: Burn them!
CHORUS: Burn them! Burn them! (*They advance to light up the bonfire.*)
AN OLD VOICE (*Blocking them.*) Stop, children! What do you think you're doing?
VOICES: Getting rid of our load.
OLD VOICE: And you think you can make it by burning up, destroying what you already have?
VOICES: Yes. What's the use of keeping them when they're worthless to us?
OLD VOICE: Your certificates? Degrees?
VOICES: Yes. Papers! Papers! Not life. And they can burn! We can't spend our entire youth waiting.
OLD VOICE (*Laughing, calming them down.*): True, I agree. It's not fair.
ANGRY VOICES: The system's not fair!
OLD VOICE (*Still smiling.*) Children, let's talk about fairness! You know how long I've been waiting here?
VOICE ONE (*Challenging.*): What? When?
OLD VOICE: Child, long before you and maybe your father and mother were born.
VOICE: TWO: You too, Baba? What the hell are you doing here?
VOICE ONE: He's applying to be a security guard.
VOICE TWO (*Laughing.*) Sure the Baba will be first.
CROWD: From behind. Yes! (*They burst out laughing.*)
VOICE TWO: Go home, old man. And rest in peace.
CROWD: In pieces!
OLD VOICE (*Delirious.*): I blame anybody? No. It's my luck. All my life, I've been waiting. In line. I've been in this God-forsaken place waiting. Hoping against hope just to get my turn. But here I am still, struggling and trying to find my way...my place among these young people that are not even as old as my youngest child. Is it their fault? No? But the government? This government? These rulers? Long before some of them were born, I started serving this country. Even forced to fight,

for I-don't-know-who now in Burma...India. Yes! I did. And that was still when I was a young man. Yes, me too. Young. Young. Do they remember? Does anyone remember that now? No? But I do. (*Voice cracking.*) Yes. I spent my entire youth serving this country. And now...

A VOICE: But Baba, we the youth today are just asking, waiting for an opportunity to serve.

A VOICE: Don't interrupt the old man. Let him speak!

ANOTHER: The youths today have no respect for anybody. Old Baba go on. Let's hear your story.

A VOICE: His complaint!

ANGRY VOICES: Shut up! Let the old man speak! ( *Brief silence.*)

CROWD: Yes, Baba. Speak. We're listening!

OLD VOICE (*Clearing his throat.*) Then I came back from the war, joined the railway company. Worked and worked until I was tired...with the promise that we'll all get our pension. Ask me where that pension is now? Ask, children. Where is my pension? Why am I, an old man of 65 years standing here, fighting my way with hundreds of you to interview for a security job that will only be given to one person? Just one single person...One single job for a whole community? (*ATLANTIC and KAINJI suddenly reemerge. They're heavily armed. KAINJI orders 99% of them to step aside.*)

NIGER: See? E troway me because I be woman.

OJI/OLD MAN: No. Na because you be old woman.

NIGER (*Vexed.*): I old pass you?

OJI/Old Man: No curse me-o.

ATLANTIC (*Angry.*): Quiet!

MOB (*Banging at the gate.*): Open! Open the gate!

ATLANTIC: You're trespassing.

MOB: Who?

ATLANTIC: All of you. This is private property.

MOB: In our land.

ATLANTIC (*Screaming.*) Now silence! (*The rumbling and shoving decrease somewhat. But each one displaced is still struggling for place and prominence.*)

KAINJI: Do you hear me?

MOB: Noooooooo! (*ATLANTIC and KAINJI again confer and retreat into the villa.*)

KAINJI: Now silence. The Director speaks!

MOB LEADER: Director of wetin?

A VOICE: Director of hunger!
VOICES (*Chanting.*): Director of Death! Homelessness! Director of Unemployment.
MOB CHORUS: Jobless! Jobless! Jobless!
MOB LEADER: Director of Pollution!
MOB CHORUS: Pollution! Pollution! Pollution! Director of pollution!
MOB LEADER: You be de Managing Director?
MOB CHORUS: Hear! Hear! You Damaging Director. Hear! Hear! Hear! Hear. Damaging Director. Hear! Hear! Hear! (*The displaced crowd is so enraged they surge forward, dangerously rattling the iron gate.*)
ATLANTIC: Silence!
KAINJI: And get in line. (*They calm down as they shove and push to get in line. Each one tries to wave or brandish the certificates, degrees and whatever else they bring with them.*)
ATLANTIC (*Shouting.*): Get in line everybody. Just a simple instruction. Get in line. Order! Nothing will be done without order! (*As the crowd reorganizes itself, ATLANTIC again retreats with the Government official to plan their strategies. The people continue quarreling among themselves in the background.*)
VOICE ONE (*Struggling to make his way through.*): Don't push me. I came here before you.
VOICE TWO (*Pushing.*) Who say dat? Me, I dey wait here and wait and wait. Five years. That's how long I've been waiting to get this opportunity to stand out here in the sun and be told to shut up, instead of being given a job and allowed to work. Work! Work? Yes. I'm begging for work, not handout or charity. Look, I'm thirty something years old. Graduated from the university five years ago and still scrambling and groping for a place...a job. Is that how to be a man? When? When? When will I ever be...become a man? Imagine the waste. 6 years of my life in primary school. Five years in secondary school. Another four...five...in the university. And yet another five...six... eternal years waiting...waiting...just to be invited to an and I'm not even sure of that? (*Voice cracking.*) How? (*Tearfully.*) How long? How long? (*Sighs, starts flexing his muscles.*) Look. Look at my hands. I'm able. I can work. I can dig. I can type. I can shovel. I can read. I can write...I can... I can...(*Voice cracking.*) How? How long? How long? (*Sighing. ETHIOPE, now as Old Man shoves himself forward and takes the center-stage.*)
OLD MAN: Child, you ask me again? (*Silence.*) Look at me. You see my head? (*Taking off his cap and showing it to the crowd.*) Now, count.

Count the grey on my head and guess how long I've been waiting? (*Silence.*) For life! (*Hysterical laughter.*) If you children are complaining about waiting for the better life? Now look who's talking? What about me?
ANOTHER VOICE (*Surging forward.*): What about me?
OTHER VOICES: Wetin? What about *we*?
CHORUS: Us?
VOICE ONE: Go siddon! You people came late.
OLDER VOICES: And we parents? What about the parents?
OLDER MAN: Oh children. You'll never know how much weighs on the back of parents!
OLDER VOICES: We parents. Without money, without power, without without without...
OLDER MAN: Yes. You feel less than a man.
OLDER WOMAN: And as woman?
WOMEN: You feel less. And less. (*Mock laughter.*)
OLDER VOICES: And what about parents?
OLDER VOICES: You feel-you feel less. And LESS!
OLDER MAN: Oh, children! You'd never know how we long to be men.
YOUNGER VOICE (*OBIDA, stepping forward.*) And women! (*Screaming.*) Hear us, you who abuse us!
ANOTHER VOICE: And she said it!
MOB: Hear ! Hear! Hear, you who abuse us!
YOUNGER VOICES: What about us?
OLDER VOICES: Time...
YOUNGER VOICES: Time is us! Now!
OLDER VOICES: And we? What do we do? What should parents do?
A YOUNG VOICE (*Perhaps OBIDA?*) Speak, parents! Let the parents speak! (*The mob breaks into a chant.*)
MOB (*Clamoring and drumming.*): Let the parents speak! Let our parents speak! Hear them-hear them-hear them speak! Hear them speak! Hear them speak! (*In this charged and heated ground, ATLANTIC re-emerges with the Government Official. Pointing in a certain direction of the crowd, the allies confer.* )
ATLANTIC (*Nodding.*): Ok. I hear. (*KAINJI sifts through the crowd and eliminates more women and the old men that he orders to step aside.*)
KAINJI (*Departing.*): It's time. I've got to be at the security meeting.
ATLANTIC: Hurry up now. (*With the help of the Government Official, the eliminated ones are ordered out of the premises. ATLANTIC inspects the preliminary list of candidates. KAINJI/ Government Official now*

*disappears through the door behind the lounge. But he quickly reappears, masked, dressed in a sparkling white long sleeve shirt, a pair of trousers, shoes and tie to march. Reappearing as one of the candidates, he joins the cue. ATLANTIC, the oil director picks him out.)*
ATLANTIC: You, follow me. (*He obeys. ATLANTIC hands him a baton, a gun, hand cuffs, and a red uniform. Protests, shouts and more anger from those rejected.)*
ATLANTIC: You're hired. (*KAINJI bows.*) The rest of you? Fired! (*To KAINJI.*) Guard, get them out of here.
KAINJI/GUARD): When you finish?
ATLANTIC: Now, idiot!
KAINJI/GUARD (*Military salute.*): Yes saar! (*He orders them to leave but they resist.)*
ATLANTIC: Shoot any offender at sight.
KAINJI/GUARD (*Fidgeting.*) Ye...ye...saar! *(In panic, he tries to pull the trigger but he's too nervous to make an impact. The Guard begins to push them away. Another tug of war begins.)*
A VOICE: You see? They've hired again from another tribe. But we're here. They won't employ us.
ANOTHER VOICE: Who are we? Do we count?
VOICES: Oga Director, is it fair? Is it fair? Right inside our own land. Right here in our own land. Oga, is it fair?
ATLANTIC (*From his distance.*): No apologies folks! Ask your government. I have a contract. It's my bargain with your government. (*Reads.*) "Hire those who would best protect your interest. For compensation, see the owners of the land." And that we have done!
A VOICE: Na lie! They took my own land.
ANOTHER VOICE: And drilled oil right inside my own farmland. Now I have no where to farm. And you leveled my rubber plantation.
A VOICE: How long? How long? (*Echoes of 'how long' fill the air. The protesters still resist even as the Guard threatens to shoot at them. As they chant their protests, they form a human shield in a circle, then break into a soulful tune. The new Guard shouts his orders for them to leave but they wouldn't budge. ATLANTIC returns, orders them out but they refuse. Instead, they begin to throw rotten tomatoes, eggs, missiles, anything they can get hold of until ATLANTIC retreats to the door and yells his final order.)*
ATLANTIC : Shoot at sight! (*Still in panic, the Guard pulls the trigger. A young man falls. Commotion, stampede as the mob flees in different directions, while some carry the fallen, shoulder high, as they sing a dirge.)*

VOICE of OBIDA (*Threatening.*): We will not be silenced!
CHORUS OF VOICES: We will retaliate!
VOICE OF OBIDA: Oh, yes. We will.
CHORUS OF VOICES: Retaliate! Retaliate! Retaliate!  You just get ready. Ready! Ready!!
VOICE OF OBIDA: Your people must pay.
CHORUS OF VOICES: Pay! Pay! Pay!  Their people must pay!
   ( *They sing, circle until blackout.*)

# MOVEMENT EIGHT

(*OSHUN steals back into the GRA/Oil Club with her lover, the guard. They quickly grab ATLANTIC's loaded briefcase, put on his coat, and go into hiding. ATLANTIC returns from his meeting. He is visibly agitated, smoking and pacing up and down until the Government Official and the Chief arrive for their meeting. Long Silence.*)

GOVERNMENT OFFICIAL: Tell us why you sent for us.
ATLANTIC (*Really agitated.*): To warn you...us... Things have taken a dangerous turn. Stay on high alert.
CHIEF & GOVERNMENT OFFICIAL: What? How? (*Silence. Only ATLANTIC's smoke is floating.*)
ATLANTIC: Something terrible. Terrorism. We are losing. The profit margin is sliding down. I've just read the annual fiscal report. We made only three trillion...
CHIEF (*Wide-eyed.*): Three what?
GOVERNMENT OFFICIAL: Trillion, he said.
ATLANTIC: Yes. Mere three trillion. That's all we made this year. Bare. A Bare Market. (*Sighs.*) Tell me, what are we going to do?
CHIEF: With three trillion?
ATLANTIC: Hey, Chief! Watch out. I'm serious. (*He steps inside.*)
GOVERNMENT OFFICIAL: He means business.
CHIEF: I see. (*ATLANTIC returns with documents that he shares with his partners.*)
ATLANTIC: You see? Much below expectation, at least compared to the double digit profit for last year and also projected for this year.
CHIEF: Well, things do change.
ATLANTIC: I know. But at whose expense? (*Silence.*) Yes, tell me. Who pays for the change? You? Me? Us?
CHIEF & GOVERNMENT OFFICIAL (*Screams.*): I guess not.
ATLANTIC: Then do. Do something!
GOVERNMENT OFFICIAL: We have to.
ATLANTIC (*Screams.*): Our investments are not safe.
CHIEF: And lives too!
ATLANTIC: Ahaa! Now you said it! Fear...I'm afraid... (*Pauses, takes a deep breath.*) But how can anyone invest in a land that's so unstable? The primary rule of capital investment? Stability. Stability. Stability! And that's grossly lacking here. Just in the last month alone, with their

riots, we've lost three million. Isn't that enough loss... sacrifice for us to give to this God damn country? I mean...excuse my language. But I stand by the truth. And I'm really getting sick of...
*(Makes a dash for the room again and doesn't hear the rest.)*
CHIEF: The truth?
GOVERNMENT OFFICIAL: The whole mess.
CHIEF: Country...
GOVERNMENT OFFICIAL: Your business. *(Pause.)* Why can't we agree on anything?
CHIEF: Our way...?
GOVERNMENT: Yes. Right! So what is new?
ATLANTIC *(Returning, stomping his cigarette.):* What is *not* new?
CHIEF & GOVERNMENT OFFICIAL: That is the question!
ATLANTIC: There's always something... something, always. And now they have the guts to come to a director's home to rob...
CHIEF: Which?
CHIEF & GOVERNMENT OFFICIAL *(Alarmed.):* Who dared?
ATLANTIC: Who else? *Your* noble people, of course!
GOVERNMENT OFFICIAL: I'm so sorry about this development.
CHIEF: Me too.
ATLANTIC: You better be. Especially you, Chief. Your people are getting quite unruly. Warn...restrain them. Because I won't take any shit from those blasted idiots. I too I'm going on the offensive.
CHIEF: We can...not...
ATLANTIC *(Ignores him and starts to parody the indigenous people's accent.)* "Our people are suffering-Our people are suffering...Suffering... Suffering...No jobs-no jobs?" Am I responsible? What is my business if they can't feed? And why should they if all they do is spend time, valuable time making trouble instead of money?
CHIEF: But how will they make money if...
ATLANTIC *(Furious.):* Then let them go and work. Find jobs!
CHIEF: But it's not that easy.
ATLANTIC: Yes. Control. We've lost...
CHIEF: We're trying...
ATLANTIC: To lose it. That's what you're doing.
CHIEF: No. Believe me, director. Everything's being done to...
ATLANTIC: Liquidate us.
GOVERNMENT OFFICIAL: Oh, no!
CHIEF: Far from it, director. The people are getting only more and more agitated.
ATLANTIC *(Sarcastically.):* Any other news?

CHIEF: Hnm...well...
ATLANTIC: Say it.
CHIEF: They still need...
ATLANTIC (*Furious.*): Jobs! Job! Jobs!
CHIEF: Food. Electricity! Water!
ATLANTIC: Hello! The people's Solicitor and Advocate! I'm not in their way. Am I?
Chief: No...Who can say...Ehm...(*Coughs.*)
ATLANTIC: That's the sea right there. It's completely open to them. Fish or drown, I'm not in anybody's way. Or are they claiming there's water shortage in the sea too?
CHIEF (*Fidgeting.*): Oh no. How can? Just...just that they can't drink sea water. Nobody does.
ATLANTIC: Hey! Wait a minute, Chief. On whose side are you?
CHIEF: Yours! *(They laugh.)*
ATLANTIC: Then maybe your people need to start importing water from abroad. After all, you import nearly everything else, even the fuel...
GOVERNMENT OFFICIAL: But that's only temporary. Our refineries have all broken down.
ATLANTIC: Your excuse?
GOVERNMENT OFFICIAL: Importing fuel is the only option. At least for now.
ATLANTIC (*Sarcastically.*): Thanks for the information. But I must tell you. I hate people blaming others. And you people are just so good at that.
GOVERNMENT OFFICIAL: The simple solution is to...
CHIEF: Create more jobs
GOVERNMENT OFFICIAL: And more...
ATLANTIC: Did I not employ a guard only...?
CHIEF: Well, that's just one. I mean...the people are suffering.
ATLANTIC (*Mock laughter.*): Their mantra! Yes, their claim to fame! Bravo! Su-ffe-ring. Su-ffe-ring! Africa's other name!
GOVERNMENT OFFICIAL: It doesn't take much. Just something. If only we'd appear to be doing something.
ATLANTIC: If you say so.
CHIEF: I know my people.
ATLANTIC: But do they know you?
CHIEF: We need to cover...
ATLANTIC: How?
GOVERNMENT: Our tracks. Jobs. I mean...(*Coughs.*)
CHIEF: More jobs!

ATLANTIC: Ok, then. What?
GOVERNMENT: Employ more cooks, stewards, gardeners, janitors etc.
ATLANTIC: That's more salaries and benefits to pay. The stake keeps getting higher and higher every day. How are we going to pay for all that excess?
GOVERNMENT OFFICIAL: Hire them part-time. No...(*Pause.*) Still problematic. No. (*Pensive.*) Maybe we'll just drill more oil. Sell more barrels per day. And with some OPEC members bought...I mean...competing against each other...
ATLANTIC (*Ecstatic.*): Great! Always a good idea to pump more crude. I like that.
GOVERNMENT OFFICIAL: Certainly means more oil glut...for us.
ATLANTIC: Too bad. It's the price of the game. Don't take it personally. You'll make up anyway. You both.
GOVERNMENT OFFICIAL (*Winking at ATLANTIC.*): Well, after...
CHIEF (*Winking at ATLANTIC.*) We'll talk.
ATLANTIC: Still on this business, huh? (*His eyes suddenly light up as he rises.*) Yes, I got the answer!
CHIEF: What?
GOVERNMENT: Tell us!
ATLANTIC (*Grabs the map hanging by the wall. He shows it to them.*) You see this?
CHIEF & GOEVERNMENT OFFICIAL: The bridge to the pipeline?
ATLANTIC: It's strategic. We know that. Don't we?
CHIEF & GOVERNMENT: Yes!
ATLANTIC: Now. We've just built an expressway linking the inland with the offshore line. And it's a lot of traffic. Traders traveling to buy and sell, you know?
CHIEF & GOVERNMENT: Yes.
ATLANTIC: Ok, That's it. That's the answer! We'll just erect a toll gate here on this spot. (*Pointing.*) The junction between this 'crude state' and this refinery spot. With the tolls collected from the people we can create employment for the villagers on both sides of the river and pay their salary too.
GOVERNMENT OFFICIAL: A great idea. Except these insatiable crooks. They'll print their own tickets anyway. Sell half for government and half for themselves.
CHIEF: Then collect more.
GOVERNMENT OFFICIAL: You'd be lucky if they give you any receipts. They'll keep telling motorists that they've run out of receipts. So

what do we do?
ATLANTIC: Then don't pay the damn...Don't take it. No pay without receipts!
CHIEF (*Laughing.*) My friend, you really don't know how the system works. 'No business, no show.'
GOVERNMENT OFFICIAL: As the girls say nowadays. "Money for hand, back na ground!"
CHIEF: "No honey, no money!" I've heard that too. (*They laugh.*)
GOVERNMENT OFFICIAL: Seriously, it sounds like a good idea.
ATLANTIC: And more. We have better security. A new checkpoint will be added.
CHIEF: And a canteen too, where the workers can eat.
GOVERNMENT OFFICIAL: And the women can find jobs as cooks. I personally would need cleaners, janitors.
GOVERNMENT OFFICIAL: Me too. I'll need more domestic-help.
ATLANTIC: Sure. Our pets are lonely...just too lonely. You know, Dr. Vet recently made a major discovery...(*Pause.*) That Hero...my Hero...is suffering from depression.
GOVERNMENT OFFICIAL: Your dog, too?
ATLANTIC: Yes. Poor thing. Abused. Abused. We must protect their rights.
CHIEF: Animals...
ATLANTIC: Precious pe... Handle with care. Your people better be warned. I'll kill for my pet. Your people better be warned. Handle with care. (*Excited as he sells the idea now.*) Pets. Dogs...man's very best friend. Trust them. Train them as security guards. Much more reliable, I tell yah. Give them a Clinic too. You know this year alone, many have died from cholera? No clean water.
CHIEF: Too bad for them...
ATLANTIC (*Fiercely.*): For us!
CHIEF: I have a great idea.
GOVERNMENT OFFICIAL: Build industries to create jobs.
ATLANTIC: Nonsense!
GOVERNMENT OFFICIAL: Far too expens...
ATLANTIC: Expensive, yes! And who's to pay for all that?
CHIEF: Who else but you...
ATLANTIC: Don't be silly, Chief. You mean I came here to serve... (*Rising with a spark in his eyes.*) Look Gentlemen. You know what? I got the solution. (*The others listen attentively.*) A great idea. Your people would be better served if we had a nursery.
CHIEF & GOVERNMENT OFFICIAL: Oh yes, a nursery! Their children...
ATLANTIC: Our dogs!

CHIEF (*Alarmed.*) : What?
ATLANTIC: Our pets are suffering. Cabin fever. We work too hard. Too long and not enough time to give them quality care. And these pets are really the only true friends... companions that we have in the field. (*Pause.*) We need to protect our own. Build a nursery for them.
CHIEF: Yes, but...
ATLANTIC: Just listen to me. A pet house will cost much less.
CHIEF (*Laughing.*) Oh yes. Rather reminds me of a joke I heard from a friend about an African woman who was trying to rent a house in America. The Landlord required that she fill out long forms to prove herself, her assets, her credit worthiness and all that. And you know those Americans? Just as we do...I tell you, those people don't joke with their penny. Money? *Their* life. Ha! (*Bucolic laughter.*)
GOVERNMENT OFFICIAL: So what happened to the African woman?
CHIEF: My friend said that everything was ok, until the she was about to append her signature to the lease and then the Landlord asked, "By the way, Miss, do you have kids?" And thinking that her children were her great assets, the woman proudly relied, "Oh yes. Four. I'm blessed with four children." Immediately, the Landlord's face turned red. He rose, tore up the lease and showed the woman to the door. "Sorry Mam. I can't rent my house to you. Pets ok. No kids." "Wh... wha...What?" the stunned woman managed to cry out. "I repeat. Pets ok. No kids! Goodbye!" The Landlord slammed the door in her face.
ATLANTIC: And that's right.
CHIEF: Whose?
GOVERNMENT OFFICIAL (*Chuckling.*): Let's face it...
ATLANTIC (*Ignoring them.*): I know a good Vet-Doctor in Texas. Hire him.
GOVERNMENT OFFICIAL: But we still need something...Something more...
CHIEF: Like a general hospital for the people?
ATLANTIC: We can't afford it.
CHIEF: But we afford one for dogs?
ATLANTIC (*Furious.*): Yes, sir! Who's going to pay for a general hospital? You'll need to hire more specialized professional staff, fringe benefits, doctors, nurses, lab technicians, aids and more.
GOVERNMENT OFFICIAL (*Drinking.*): I see with you. The more skilled workers, the higher the salary. Benefits. Retirement benefits. Worker's compensation. Housing. It's true. We can't afford it now (*The Chief turns away in silence.*)
ATLANTIC: Great! Great reasoning, my friend! The less committed we are to these people, the better. So I propose that all future employment

that we offer be part-time. Temporary. Gives us the flexibility and controlling edge. (*To Chief.*) Your silence troubles... I mean are you with me?
CHIEF (*Startled.*): Oh yes. Too much with you. Just thinking...
ATLANTIC (*Calmly.*) What now, Chief?
CHIEF (*Winking at ATLANTIC.*): You and I can make...make a deal... I mean ehnm...work together.
ATLANTIC: Of course! Of course! (*Silence as the Government Official f tries to make the rest of the deal with his eyes.*) Produce more jobs. There's more than enough care to go around. You agree?
GOVERNMENT OFFICIAL: Sure! Some will walk the dogs in the morning. Others will have to walk them in the evening.
CHIEF: Hnm... But a full time job just for dog care? People are going to think it's insulting.
ATLANTIC (*Chuckling.*): As if they're any better!
GOVERNMENT OFFICIAL: We'll stress that we need those dogs for security.
ATLANTIC (*Fist salute.*): Thanks. Friends, thank you! And the sooner, the better.
CHIEF (*Looks at his partners.*): So it's a deal?
GOVERNMENT OFFICIAL: If *we* say so.
ATLANTIC: And it is!
GOVERNMENT OFFICIAL (*Smacking his lips, saluting the Chief playfully.*): Man no die!
CHIEF: Man no rotten!
GOVERNMENT OFFICIAL: Do we have a choice?
CHIEF: I guess not.
GOVERNMENT OFFICIAL: We're together.
CHIEF (*Winking at him.*): Till *they* do us part! (*They all laugh.*)
ATLANTIC (*Drinks, seals the deal.*): We'll start immediately. And the pet nursery shall be called, "The New Haven."
CHIEF: The Holy place?
ATLANTIC: Yes. Most sacred.
GOVERNMENT OFFICIAL: A New Haven for dogs and cats?
ATLANTIC: Sure. Now you're talking! Gentlemen, let's drink to that! (*Toasts.*)
(*They all laugh. Chief rises, winks again at ATLANTIC.*)
CHIEF: Our deal.
ATLANTIC: My seal.
GOVERNMENT OFFICIAL: It's time.
CHIEF (*Leaving.*): We'll see later then. (*Exit Chief. ATLANTIC disappears*

*behind the door, returns with a sign/bill board which he hands over to the Government Official to put up the sign. Suddenly, the masked youths emerge from their hiding and leap into the space. In panic, ATLANTIC fires at the nearest one. OSHUN's lover falls, injured. OSHUN flees. Lights fade out on ATLANTIC as he stares at the wounded youth, who's pleading for help and life. "Don't kill me. Please! Please!" Finally, ATLANTIC stoops, starts dragging the wounded boy away until lights fade out. Flute sounds in the background.)*

# MOVEMENT NINE

*(It's twilight. OBIDA in the market square, chanting invocations to her ancestors to rise up and come to their aid.)*

OBIDA: Rise up, mothers! My ancestors. Wake! Wake. Wake up! Your daughters need you now. The tide is high, high up. The flood threatens to swallow us. And sharks, white and black, have taken over the shores. Our land. Arise mothers! Your daughters are sinking. Drowning. Gobbled as torn flesh by the ever hungry sharks now ruling our land. *(Desperately.)* Can't you hear me? Mothers, arise! Lead us! *(She's crying so loud, the other women and youths are alarmed and begin to arrive at the market square. They declare a Town Meeting. NIGER rouses and addresses the gathering.)*

NIGER: Mothers, sons and daughters. Who owns this land?

CHORUS: We own the land!

NIGER: I say who owns this land?

CHORUS: We own the land!

NIGER: I say who?

CHORUS: We!

NIGER: Who?

CHORUS: We!

*(With them all now completely animated, NIGER clears her throat to speak.)*

NIGER: Mothers, sons and daughters of the land. It is I, NIGER. The umbilical cord, running all through these coasts from here to the Fouta Djallon mountain that speaks. You know me, I know you. I, NIGER, leader of the market-place. Appointed by you, women of this land to lead you with the assistance of sister BENUE. But this is not about me...or her. It is about us...us. Our world! Women of deltaland, you appointed us to serve you. We are here, ready. My siblings from many shores. Today, I speak to you, not about anything new or events that you're not familiar with. Something ...something strange, smelly and strong is sapping our land. Why? Why? Why? Has it always been so? What is happening to our...world...our land? *(She's choking. Those nearest to her hold her from falling. As she recovers, BENUE rises and takes over.)*

BENUE: You heard her, our sister. She said it! What did our sister say?

WOMEN: Something. Strange. Smelly-Strong is sapping our land.

BENUE: People of the land and sea. I know we all have come from different directions to meet here. We are here, now. Together. What are we going to do? As they say, if you don't lick and massage your lips, the fierce dry harmattan wind will lick it for you. People of the Delta! Our land bleeds! The land weeps! Tell me, who among you here, no matter how young, no matter how old, has not lost our blood?
CHORUS: All! All of us!
BENUE: Your fathers and brothers?
CHORUS: Lost. Branded or wounded!
BENUE: Your mothers and sisters?
CHORUS (*Inflamed.*): Defied. Maimed or murdered!
BENUE: Your pride and dignity?
CHORUS: Cut down!
BENUE: And if they take all that away, what then is left?
CHORUS: Nothing! Nothing!
BENUE: Not even the land is left. Not taken... Not polluted.
CHORUS: Nothing! Nothing!
BENUE: We're taken.
CHORUS: Taken. Taken. Taken!
BENUE: Ever since they discovered oil in our land, they drill, dry, and fry us alive with the fishes and farmlands all cooking in the oil.
CHORUS: The oil. Our oil!
BENUE: So what will become of us...our children? (*Pause.*) Do you smell the decaying bodies of husbands, sons and daughters?
CHORUS: Yes!
BENUE: Do you smell the fishes roasting in their hot oil poured over the rivers?
CHORUS: Yes! They've refined our oil into a curse!
BENUE: Where? Where else in the world does oil cease to anoint?
CHORUS: Here! Here! Here!
BENUE: Plants, animals, children, men, women cooking in their oil. Oil sapped from the very soul of our sagging land. Ah! People of the delta! Do you see yourselves drowning?
CHORUS: Yes!
BENUE: Starving?
CHORUS: Yes!
BENUE: Wilting?
CHORUS: Yes!
BENUE: What then are you waiting for, mothers, sons and daughters? (*In this fury, the mob rises, facing the direction of the GRA/OIL Club.*)

CHORUS: Nothing! Nothing! No more waiting!
BENUE: I do not wish to speak for you or for anybody. Let every woman speak for herself. And in the end tell us women, what are we going to do? (*Chanting*.) What are we going to do-What are we going to do- to do- to do- to doooo?
KOKO: When our land is burnt and bonded.
OBIDA: Why should you when you have your army to fight your wars?
KOKO: Why should you stand still, your voices choking when you are the oil and the river?
OBIDA: When you are the heart and breast of the land?
CHORUS: Yes! Yes! She said it! Said it! Yes, she said it!
OBIDA: Why? why? Why, mothers, sons and daughters of the delta?
CHORUS: Why-why-why?
OBIDA: Who can silence the drums? Delta Women Speak!
CHORUS: Yes! Here we are. Ready! (*OBIDA breaks into military steps. They follow as they sing and dance in circles:*
**Onye Akpana nwa agu aka nodu.**
NIGER: Onye Akpana Nwagu aka nodu
CHORUS OF WOMEN: M'Odin ndu. Onwu la nwu!
NIGER: Onye Akapana Nwagu Akano du
CHORUS OF WOMEN: M'Odin ndu. M'Onwu la Nwu!
NIGER: Onye Akpana, Nwa gu aka nodu.
CHORUS OF WOMEN: M' odi ndu. Onwu la nuu! (*The women have risen into this frenzied dance, when suddenly, OSHUN appears, covered in a white shroud.*)
OBIDA: (*Excitedly*.): Look who's here! (*Sudden hush.*)
NIGER (*Breathless*.): My child! My life! (*Grips OSHUN.*)
OBIDA: Where have you been? (*All the women surround OSHUN, who is still panting.*)
NIGER: So you are alive, my daughter?
OSHUN (*Panting*.): Ye...ye...Yes. But...
BENUE: Tell us what happened? Where is my son?
OSHUN: They...got... got... Took him.
BENUE (*Alarmed*.): Dead?
OSHUN: Alive. But captive.
BENUE (*Frantic*.): Where? Tell...tell me...us!
OSHUN: In jail. Their cell. But he'll return. He's strong. And he tells me to tell you not to give up. You must continue to fight. Fight! (*Still gasping.*) The ba...battle has just...just... begun. Mothers get ready! Sisters get ready.

OBIDA: What did she say?
CHORUS OF WOMEN: Mothers. Sisters. Get ready! Ready! Ready!
KOKO: And she said it!
CHORUS OF WOMEN: Get ready! Ready! Ready!
OSHUN: Are you ready?
CHORUS OF WOMEN: Yes! *(They start pulling off their headwraps to reinforce the wrappers around their waists. They grab stumps and broken branches and twigs. Suddenly, OSHUN bursts into laughter, as she watches the women. Shocked, they freeze.)*
OSHUN *(Still laughing.)*: Mothers and sisters. You're not going to fight men with guns and bullets with your bare hands and twigs? *(Still frozen, the women look from one to the other.).* No mothers and sisters. We cannot. Must not play their bloody game. For that is what they are. BLOODY!
BENUE: So daughter, tell us. How should we fight?
CHORUS OF WOMEN: How? How are we going to fight their guns?
OBIDA: Our soul. United...
KOKO: Again she said it!
CHORUS OF WOMEN: Our souls! Our spirits! Fight! Fight!
OSHUN *(Rousing them.)*: Wounded or healed?
CHORUS OF WOMEN: Fight! Fight! We'll fight! *(They chant until OBIDA drowns their voices with the vibrant drums of the congo music that she plays to electrify the crowd. As if called to action, their feet step up. They hold each other and break up into two concentric circles; the daughters on the one hand, and the mothers on the other. OSHUN now leads the daughters, while NIGER leads the mothers until the circles merge into one. Then OSHUN halts them all as she unfolds to them the secret plans she's heard from the Oil Club.)*
OSHUN: I know the white oil director. He's planning to go on leave to America. They go every ten weeks you know. There they spend five weeks "to recover from the abuse of the weather in Africa," they say. *(Chuckles.)*
NIGER: Running? Let them!
CHORUS OF WOMEN: Just wait. Wait. Our daughters are coming!
OSHUN *(Turning to her mother.):* Mother, I'm sorry I didn't listen to you. But I'm glad, too, because by not obeying you, I too have learned. Now I know better. Forgive, forgive mothers and sisters. *(They embrace each other. The women break into song and serenade, until OSHUN again intervenes.)*
OSHUN: Mothers and daughters of the delta!

CHORUS OF WOMEN: Eeeih!
OSHUN: I get tori. (*Immediately, the women rally round her in a half moon shape as she declares: 'story- story'?*)
CHORUS OF WOMEN: 'Story'!
OSHUN: Mothers and daughters of deltaland. Open your eyes and ears. Get ready. The thing we have been looking for in Sokoto, we now find in our *shokoto*!
CHORUS OF WOMEN (*Excitedly.*): Go on! Tell us! Show us! We are ready!
OSHUN (*Smiles, confides in them.*): You know wetin?
CHORUS: No!
OSHUN: I heard many things in our hideout. After KAINJI was shot and taken away, I had no way to escape. And with that whitemen threatening with his gun, ready to shoot anyone pointblank, I got scared. Very scared and crept under those big chairs they sit on to drink whisky and brandy in their club. Then the Chief, and later the Government Official came to see the whiteman to plan as usual (*Pause.*): My mothers and sisters, if you know what these people think? What they're planning for us? You'll weep.
CHORUS OF WOMEN: Say it!
BENUE: Dead body no be new tin for ground. Tell us!
OSHUN: You really want to know?
CHORUS OF WOMEN: Yes!
OSHUN: Then get ready.
CHORUS OF WOMEN: We are.
OSHUN: Now hear it. They're putting a toll-gate on that bridge linking our land across the rivers. (*Awaits their reaction.*)
NIGER: And so?
BENUE: Yes! You know. They're always mounting walls, roads and bridges.
OBIDA: Not for our own development but for moving their oil and goods from our land overseas. So it's just another bridge from our land to their pockets.
NIGER: And that brings me to my question. What is in this for us?
CHORUS OF WOMEN: Yes. What is in it for us?
OSHUN (*Smiling.*): Now listen. They say they will employ our people to collect money at the toll-gate.
CHORUS OF WOMEN: Good! Now they're talking. There will be free flow of money in our hands!
OSHUN: And you know that road is so busy?
CHORUS OF WOMEN: Yes!
BENUE: But the tickets sold belong to them.

OSHUN: Are we going to be fools forever?
CHORUS: Nooooo!
OSHUN: Are we going to be used forever?
CHORUS: No! No! No!
OBIDA: How monkey go dey work-work-work and baboon go dey chop?
CHORUS OF WOMEN: No more! Who born monkey?
OSHUN: No! Dem never born am!
BENUE: We don tire for dem monkey business.
KOKO: She said it!
CHORUS: We tire! Tire! We don tire!
OSHUN: So?
OBIDA: We too go begin sell our own tickets!
BENUE: 'Shikena,' as our northern brothers and sisters say.
CHORUS: That's it. So be it!
OSHUN & OBIDA: Who owns this land afterall?
CHORUS OF WOMEN: We! We! Our land! We must-must take back what is ours! (*Chanting.*) Resource Control! Resource Control!
OSHUN (*Sing-Song manner.*): And that is just the beginning. Something, something else is going to happen.
CHORUS: Tell us! Tell us daughter, tell us!
OSHUN (*Smiles mischievously, then screams.*): Mothers and daughters of the delta!
CHORUS OF WOMEN: Eeih!
OSHUN: Your leaders...
CHORUS OF WOMEN: We have no leaders. Away with leaders!
OBIDA: We're tired of being mis-led.
KOKO (*Stepping forward.*): By the nose?
CHORUS OF WOMEN: Enough! We reject all leaders of falsehood. We reject leaders that take and take and never give anything good in return. Away! Away with their lies!
NIGER: But caution, children.
BENUE: Yes, easy.
NIGER: As our people say, "there will be enough sleep for the dead in the grave."
BENUE: That is if they let you die in peace.
NIGER: And even when you die, will they let you be buried? Sleep? That is the question! Some of us are worth more dead than alive...
OBIDA: Buried alive.
NIGER: Some of us are worth nothing dead or alive!
OBIDA: That too must end. Trust us mothers. Times are changing. We, your

daughters are here.
NIGER: She said it! Said it!
CHORUS OF MOTHERS: Our daughters are here! Speak! Speak daughters!
(*OSHUN steps forward again to the center.*)
OSHUN: Now the big news!
CHORUS OF WOMEN: We can't wait. We'll show them! We can't wait!
OSHUN: Now hear what our mis-leaders are saying.
CHORUS: We're all ears.
OSHUN: Tomorrow, they're converting the Boys Quarters in their Club into a Nursery Day-Care center.
CHORUS OF WOMEN: For whom?
NIGER: Their children of course!
OSHUN (*Smiling.*): No mother. For their Dogs!
CHORUS (*Stunned.*): Dogs?
OSHUN: Yes. A day-care nursery for their pets and puppies.
OBIDA (*Carrying an imaginary banner.*): Welcome to the nursery. Pets, ok. No kids!
CHORUS: Ha! Ha!Ha!
OSHUN (*Crying an imaginary microphone.*): You got insurance?
CHORUS: For dogs and puppies! (*They laugh.*)
CHORUS: So what else?
OBIDA: What else is new in this their new world order?
NIGER: What else is in it for us?
BENUE: That is what we want to know.
CHORUS: Tell us! Tells us!
OSHUN: You know, last time that Oyibo Shame director traveled home on leave? He came back and complained bitterly that his pet dog looked emaciated and emotionally disturbed because of loneliness and lack of care. His colleague, the other oil director from....you-know-what...?
CHORUS: Yes.
OSHUN: Well, he too was very bitter about his Lady Cat's condition. The cat had littered four kittens while he was drilling on-shore...off-shore post. He complained that his beloved Lady Cat and kittens were so badly neglected. He'll never forgive his house-keeper. So he fired him. And now his friend, I know only too well, vows he won't take it lying down. He's taken his 'Hero'...
BENUE: Whose hero?
NIGER: The dog. His Hero. Listen!
BENUE: I see.

OSHUN: Mother, you never see. The director has since entrusted that dog to a psychiatrist who said the dog was suffering from acute depression. So to heal their guilt and anger, the oil directors, with the government official have met and now want to take serious action to protect their beloved pets against such habitual abuse and negligence. So now they're renovating the recreation area in the GRA/Oil Club. The place will be well furnished and maintained as a daycare center for their animal pets. Mothers and sisters! You should see the clothes, toys and food these strange people use to feed their animal pets! (*Showing.*) And they kiss the animal mouth-to-mouth.
NIGER: Our eyes will not see corruption!
CHORUS: Abomination! Abomination! Abomination! They oppress us with their pet animals.
OBIDA: They hate us and love their beloved beasts!
OSHUN: Mothers and sisters. The time has come.
OBIDA: We hear you.
KOKO: And she said it!
CHORUS OF WOMEN: The time has come!
OSHUN: If there is anything I've learned from hanging around these people, it's what is of most and least value to them. They love their money. And pets, in that order.
NIGER: Those 'hell' people..
OSHUN: Shame, mother?
OBIDA: I saw that in their own country. They'll sure kill for anything they love.
NIGER: Now what about us?
OSHUN and OBIDA: Ha! Ha! Ha! You and me?
CHORUS OF WOMEN: Yes! What about us? What do we mean to those people?
KOKO & OSHUN: Nothing. Nothing. We don't count.
OBIDA: And what about our own people in government?
OSHUN & KOKO: Ha! We don't count. Except when they want to use us.
OBIDA: First we'll deal with their hearts. I mean pets.
BENUE (*Lighting up.*): Yom-yom! Delicious 404!! We'll make soup with their dogs.
CHORUS: Yes! Yes! Kill hunger! (*They start drumming. The police appear at a distance and lay in ambush.*)
CHORUS: No more hunger!
BENUE: A full soup-pot!
NIGER (*Smacking her lips.*): My soup will be sweet. Oh so sweet. They'll smell it right from their hell camp!

OBIDA: Suya! Suya-steak! Dog meat for steak! (*They break into song and dance.*)

KOKO (*Interrupting them.*): And if we deal with the foreigners what do we do to our own?

OSHUN: Those too!

CHORUS: Yes, together.

OBIDA: To subdue our enemies. We must learn their own art. Go under. Know their secrets. And then act when they least expect it.

CHORUS: Yes! Yes! Their own art. Act when they least expect it. (*OSHUN empties the contents of the stolen briefcase.*) Here, mothers!

OSHUN: The most important weapon we need is not guns but knowledge.

OBIDA: Yes, wisdom.

OSHUN: The weapon to conquer our enemies. We must go under.

OBIDA: Know their secrets.

OSHUN: Then act when they least expect.

CHORUS: Yes! Yes! We must act. Act! Act! Act!

BENUE: But there's no time.

OBIDA: Let's go!

NIGER: I will be their nurse!

BENUE: And I, their cleaner.

OSHUN: But then it's underlined. The applicant must be young. Must speak good English. And must be clean. Always. Mother, how are you going to do it? You can't speak English.

KOKO: We'll make them over. Come mothers, let's make you up!

NIGER: I'm ready and willing to learn. Nothing is impossible. Isn't that what our mothers taught us? Yes daughters, teach me.

BENUE: Teach us, daughters. We're ready. Ready! Ready to learn. That's what the time calls for. Parents, teach your children. Children teach your parents!

CHORUS OF DAUGHTERS: She said it! Said it!

NIGER: Now show me.

(*They demonstrate and play-act as the women are made over.*)

OSHUN: When you come in, you put on your apron and say (*In an affected oily tone.*) "Good Day, my Director! What would you like for breakfast today?"

OBIDA: "Yes, good...Hannah."

OBIDA (*Play-acting.*): Sausage and bacon with continental breakfast please? Ok?

NIGER (*Interrupting.*): Saucer... and baker...?

OSHUN: You know, like Hot Dog?

OBIDA: Oh, yes! Oh, yes, massaar. Sweet *hot-dog*! I can do it...I know!
OBIDA: Yes. Wash it well. Then roll it up.
OSHUN: Good, massaar. And...your egg? Lay it how?
OBIDA: What? Lay eggs? I don't!
OSHUN: No saar. I mean how do you like it? Sunny side up?
OBIDA: What, massar?
OSHUN: I mean the tin...Your tin, saar. Like it scrambled? Or fried?
OBIDA: Oh yes, Dog. I mean, *God*. My mind... brain...A little distracted this morning. Just go ahead and boil it...
OSHUN (*Smiling.*): Good, massar. I will boil it in no time at all. Thank you saar! Thank you saar!
OBIDA: Thank *you*! (*The women burst into laughter.*)
OSHUN: And then the rest of the ads. We want a cook for the animal daycare center.
OBIDA: I!
OSHUN: A nurse for the animal daycare...
KOKO: I!
BENUE: And the money collector at the toll gate?
OSHUN: I guess I'm the only one left. I'll do it.
OBIDA: But remember. Each one for us all.
CHORUS: Each one for everyone.
NIGER: They will see not us but our handiwork.
CHORUS: Yes! Yes! Yes! They'll feel our mighty hands.
OSHUN: Come mothers and sisters. I know the way. We've waited too long. It's our time. Now.
CHORUS OF DAUGHTERS: Mothers. Sisters. Our time. Now!
CHORUS OF MOTHERS: Lead, daughters. Lead the way. Lead us! Lead us!
(*As they march forward, their voices swell in unison as they prepare for action.*)
OBIDA: Win or lose?
NIGER & BENUE: We are ready!
CHORUS: Together.
NIGER & BENUE (*Rousing them.*): Mothers and daughters of the delta!
CHORUS: Eeeih!
NIGER: Who owns this land?
CHORUS: We own this land!
NIGER: Then take. Take back what is yours, women. (*The women drum and dance. Suddenly, siren sounds. The Police in camouflage uniform, swoop on them and handcuff NIGER and BENUE. The women struggle to be free, even as they're being chained. Everything happens so*

*fast. The music and dance stop abruptly. Silence. A deafening call from OBIDA, the women charge at the predators. The struggle intensifies. The armed men throw teargas into the crowd. The captives are led away. But soon, the mob recovers; the girls first. They rouse the women once again.)*

OBIDA: Is this the end of our journey?
CHORUS *(Thundering.)*: Noooooooooooooo!
OSHUN: Where is their nursery?
CHORUS: There! In the Oil Club! *(OSHUN leads them now.)*
OBIDA: Who lives there?
CHORUS: Dogs and Cats!
KOKO: Do they live for us to die?
CHORUS: Nooooooooo!
OSHUN: Then it's time for us to live*!*
CHORUS *(Marching.)* : It's time! Time! Time! *(Led by the OSHUN, their voices rise in song once again as they quickly march in the direction of the GRA/Oil Club. The air is soon filled with the noises/sounds of frightened animals, followed by crashing sounds, dogs barking, a clap of thunder, with lightning flashes. Blackout.)*

# MOVEMENT TEN

(*Back in the GRA/OIL Club. ATLANTIC is extremely angry. He's pacing up and down the lounge and the gate area, when the Chief arrives for another emergency meeting.*)

ATLANTIC: No I can't take it anymore. Find out. Find out who did it.
CHIEF: Did what?
ATLANTIC: My Chariot. Baby Hero. Gone! (*Sighs.*)
CHIEF: Oh, well. Thank God it's not any human...I mean they didn't kill anybody. Just the dog. They probably ate...
ATLANTIC (*Screaming.*): Stop! Stop! You Thief... I mean, Chief. Can't you, can't you see the dog is my wife...I mean life. Dammit! (*Silence.*)
CHIEF: Oh, I'm so sorry.
ATLANTIC (*Explodes.*): I don't need your sorrows! Just get them! Get those culprits. Bring them to their knees! (*Fiercely.*) And especially you, Chief...?
CHIEF: What do you want? What can I do now?
ATLANTIC: Find out. They're your people. Nobody comes from another village to commit such atrocities.
CHIEF: Director, I want to do everything possible. But I must tell you this... Remember those people you have hired from outside this region?
ATLANTIC: Yes. I am the Director, remember? My discretion. And I take no orders from anybody. Not even you, Chief ETHIOPE!
CHIEF: Your right, Director. But know this. You're...I mean they're here, in our land. That makes all the difference. I've told you time and time again, the people are angry.
ATLANTIC: Is that news?
CHIEF: They feel like outsiders. Marginalized. And denied in their own land.
ATLANTIC (*Angrily.*): Blast your fucking land. Everyone! Everything! To hell with...
CHIEF: Shame, my director... pardon. I know. What they do is pour oil and petrol on fire. But our business concern...you and me...should always be to solve these problems and remain constructive.
ATLANTIC: Just don't go there. Enough! I'm not ready for any argument now. Go! All I want is to see anyone involved in this brutal murder brought to terminal justice. Don't delay. Go!
CHIEF: Take heart. Soon, the matter will be resolved. (*Exit Chief.*)
ATLANTIC (*Alone.*): What the hell am I doing in this God forsaken land? (*He*

*grabs his suit and bowler hat, stares, throws them to the floor.)* Go...go back to Tex...? Oh, no. Forget it. The Oil... oil... No. I can't...Not now... not now... The oil. The Capital. The stakes' so high. Oh so high. We'll be the losers. Oh damn the profit! I'm frying...trying in the sizzling hot oil... *(ATLANTIC is still agonizing when the Chief returns to announce that the culprits have been found and arrested.)*

CHIEF *(Excitedly.)* We've got them. Yes! The Government Official said...

ATLANTIC: Great! Son'v-a-b...

CHIEF: Let's drink to that. *(ATLANTIC opens a bottle of whiskey, drinks.)*

CHIEF: At least now, the ground is cleared for you to take that girl.

ATLANTIC: You got her?

CHIEF: Oh yes. How soon do you need her...want her to come?

ATLANTIC: Not now. Wait. Everything now has to wait. I'm tired. Tired and fed up. *(Slumps into a chair. Sighs.)* God! Can I last one more day?

CHIEF: Just trust us. Things are not as bad as you think. In fact, everything is under control.

ATLANTIC: Alarm, you mean? Whose...

CHIEF: Oh come on, director. Be optimistic.

*(Explosive noise is heard. They listen.)*

ATLANTIC: I'll blow up anybody's brain if they mess with me.

CHIEF *(Trembling.):* No. Nobody's going to...to...mess...mess...

*(Another explosion.)*

ATLANTIC *(Nervous.):* They dare not. *(The Chief is terrified but continues to pretend and peep through the gate when the Government Official arrives.)*

GOVERNMENT: We're in deep...deep...

CHIEF: Trouble? *(The Government Official, too, is trembling.)*

ATLANTIC: What now?

GOVERNMENT OFFICIAL: Ehm...Oh, God! *(Silence.)*

CHIEF: Say. What's God's...matter, I mean...? *(Slow drumbeats outside.)*

GOVERNMENT OFFICIAL: The Texac...Vice...Deputy...

ATLANTIC: Killed?

GOVERNMENT OFFICIAL: Kidnapped!

ATLANTIC *(Hysterical.):* I knew it! I knew it! Yes! Get me out of here. Now! *(He starts packing, yells.)* Guaaarrrrd!

GUARD *(Entering, salutes.):* Yesssaaar!

ATLANTIC: What the hell is going on there?

OJI/GUARD *(Enters, trembling.):* Hell...Oga! Sh...Shame...Drum...!

ATLANTIC *(Shaking him up)*: Speak! Say what? What's going on?

OJI/GUARD: Not...Notin....Notin oga!

ATLANTIC: Then what's all that noise outside?
OJI/GUARD: Oga no be me. Na de village people. Dem burn de (h)oil...de (h)oil dey for fire.
CHIEF (*Alarmed.*): What?
ATLANTIC: What's he babbling?
GOVERNMENT OFFICIAL: He means...he means the oil...
CHIEF: The pipeline's on fire.
ATLANTIC (*Stunned.*): What? I'll be damned! (*Silence.*)
CHIEF: I told you. Those people are serious.
ATLANTIC: No! Savages! Good-for-nothing-vandals...Cursed! Forever cursed! (*He throws his bunch of keys on the floor. The Guard picks them up and stands at attention while his master runs into the chamber to arm himself.*)
CHIEF (*Talking to himself.*): Terrible...Terrorist development.
GOVERNMENT OFFICIAL: I told you. These people are going to be our ruin.
CHIEF: Arrest the situation?
GOVERNMENT OFFICIAL: The people, you mean?
CHIEF: It's time. I'm going. (*Exit Chief.*)
ATLANTIC (*Returns, combat ready.*): Details. Details! Tell me who are these terrorists? How do we find them? Where?
OJI/GUARD (*Demonstrating.*): Oga, I don talk am. De people dey mad. Dem pour petrol for de place. Bring marches. De tin catch fire. Vaaaaaam! Na so. No waste time. At all-at all! E dey burn like...like hell...
ATLANTIC (*Smoking, pacing up and down.*): Fire! Oh God... My Vice... Protect...(*Sighs.*) So who's responsible? Who?
GOVERNMENT OFFICIAL: What a waste!
ATLANTIC: What a loss! I better warn the other direct...
(*He grabs the phone and dials.*)
GOVERNMENT OFFICIAL: Who?
ATLANTIC (*Ignoring him.*): Hello! Hello! Here! The Director of Sh... (*He realizes that the phone is silent. No dial tone. He throws the phone down.*) Damn! They've cut off the line. Go immediately. Tell all the foreign Directors that today's meeting is canceled. Tell them they mustn't...shouldn't leave their stations until further notice. And the General too.... (*Government Official, leaving.*)
OJI/GUARD: I hear say dem don catch...catch....
ATLANTIC : Who now? Speak?
OJI/GUARD: De petrol oga for off-shore.
ATLANTIC: What? The Director of Mob...?

OJI/GUARD: Yes. Dat oga too.

ATLANTIC: Bastards? God!

GUARD: Yes. Dem catch am. Dat red oga. De one wey get hair like like...horse... (*Still stunned, the Government Official lingers. Like a fish out of water, ATLANTIC opens his mouth, closes it again. He is choking. Government Official helps him into a chair, goes for a drink to calm him down.*)

ATLANTIC (*Sighing.*): God! My God! They got them.

GOVERNMENT OFFICIAL: Who next?

ATLANTIC: Who knows?

OJI/GUARD (*Fanning ATLANTIC.*): Oga no worry. I don lock the gate. Dem no go fit come here. Me I go massacre them, one by one. Oga no worry. I dey for your side.

GOVERNMENT OFFICIAL: Are you sure they kidnapped the Off-Shore Oil Director?

OJI/GUARD: I see am wit my koro-koro eyes like dis. (*He demonstrates.*) Dem beat am like dis...like dem Fulani boys wey dey beat cattle namma...wey no dey gree waka. (*Imaginary whipping.*) Kaaaii!

ATLANTIC: What debacle!

OJI/GUARD: Oga wetin you talk? Make I dey call Debo Cole?

ATLANTIC: Idiot! Get out of my sight. (*Turns to the Government Official.*) Does the General know about this incident already?

GOVERNMENT OFFICIAL: Hmmm, not sure. (*Pause.*) It's time for ..for the SITREP.

ATLANTIC: Yes. The situation report! (*Government Official turns to go.*)

GOVERNMENT OFFICIAL: (*To ATLANTIC.*): I'm so sorry about this.

ATLANTIC: Away with your sorrows! I don't need them. Just go. Go tell him now! (*He stops, sighs heavily.*)

GOVERNMENT OFFICIAL: Believe me. We'll do everything in our power to arrest the situation. I promise. (*Calmly.*) For now, stay home. I'll do whatever is necessary to bring all the criminals to justice. We're in this together.

ATLANTIC: Sure. You're responsible, I know. But ...but...take care...

GOVERNMENT OFFICIAL: I will. (*Sighs.*) Everything will be over. Soon. See you.

ATLANTIC: Soon. Don't be long.

GOVERNMENT OFFICIAL: I won't. (*Exit official. ATLANTIC begins to puff away at his cigarette, while he motions to the Guard to follow the Government Official on his way to the gate.*)

GOVERNMENT OFFICIAL (*Loudly to the Guard..*): It's night already. Lock

up and don't let anyone in.
GUARD (*Saluting.*): Yessaar!
GOVERNMENT OFFICIAL: You stay in charge...in your post.
GUARD: Yes saar. (*Smiles, poses proudly.*) Me I dey for charge.
GOVERNMENT OFFICIAL: He's a stranger, remember? He's in your hands.
GUARD: Oga. I know. I know. E dey for my hand. Efery tin...efery body dey for my hand now. (*Boasting.*) Me, I dey kwa!
GOVERNMENT OFFICIAL (*Emphatically.*): Then, control. Take care of him.
*(The Guard gives him a final salute. The Government Official departs. As soon as he's gone, the Guard jumps, whistles and turns off the light. Led by OSHUN, the militants crawl nearer to their target, ATLANTIC. OSHUN positions herself f to cut off the light in preparation for ATLANTIC. As they wait, throbbing drums, mixed with loud animal sounds slash through the thick silence as ATLANTIC stands, groping and confused until lights fade out on him, followed by a loud mocking laughter.)*

# MOVEMENT ELEVEN

(*An emergency cabinet meeting in a corner of the Oil Club. Present are the Government Official, the police and the Chief. They are awaiting the arrival of the General. Masked, ATLANTIC now plays the General here. While OJI plays the First Police. OBIDA or OSHUN can play the role of the Second Police.)*

GOVERNMENT OFFICIAL: What a shame! They got the Deputy Director!
CHIEF: My brother. See me, see, trouble-o! *Dis women wan pour san-san for my garri.*
GOVERNMENT OFFICIAL: Imagine? Blasted villagers! Want to hold the entire nation to ransom? Just imagine that! *(Heavy sigh.)*
CHIEF: Women? I told you. Stubborn. Stubborn goats! (*Bugle sounds interrupt them. General enters with a stick/staff. They stand at attention.)*
GENERAL *(Furious.):* Goats? No room for goats, wild or tame in this administration. *(Shouts.)* Understand?
ALL: Yes, your Excellency!
GENERAL *(To the Chief.):* Now you! What do you know about this riot?
CHIEF *(Trembling.):* Not...your Excellency. Nothing, your Excellency.
GENERAL: And those rioters are your people. Not so?
CHIEF *(Coughs, still shivering.):* Ehnmm...Oh God I know. Our enemies... *(Rapidly.)* Yes! Our enemies....Neighbors.
GENERAL: I don't care about your damned neighbors! Just tell me what's going on. Why the whole nation is on fire. Tell me why. Or you'll be sorry for...!
CHIEF: God Almighty!
GENERAL: Hey, leave God out of this. Tell me who...!
CHIEF: My General. Those people...terrorists... enemies...want...want to ruin us.
GENERAL: Enemies? Terrorists? Who? Tell me... Name?
CHIEF *(Trembling.)* Emm... em...Women...Girls...I mean boys. All of them.
GENERAL: Your people then? You sent...
CHIEF: No, your Excellency. I didn't. God knows I didn't...
GENERAL *(Enraged.)* I say leave God out of your bloody business and talk to me! Talk to me. Didn't you send them?
CHIEF: Yes, Lord... General... I mean.. ehmmm...No...*(Sighs, stops.)*
GENERAL: I take it that you have no control over them; your bloody people. And you are the appointed Chief? Why then do you think we pay

you? Eh? (*Silence.*) Your salary...your Chieftaincy title is hereby revoked with immediate effect.
CHIEF (*Alarmed, kneels at the feet of the General.*) Ah..ah..ah.. G... Gene... general...I said it. These people...the terrorist...Wahala... Aaaaaah!
GOVERNMENT OFFICIAL: And worse still, the deputy...Vice Director...
GENERAL (*Howling.*) His Vice...? My God! What's wrong? Tell me what happened?
GOVERNMENT OFFICIAL: Kid...
GENERAL (*Hysterical.*) Nabbed?
GOVERNMENT OFFICIAL: Napped...General...Kidnapped. That's what I meant.
GENERAL: Foreign nationals? Partners kidnapped? This country? Nonsense!
GOVERNMENT OFFICIAL: Yes, General. Beats me...
GENERAL: And now we can't drill or sell oil. Losses! Losses! And more losses! (*Silence.*) Now let's hear the full report.
GOVERNMENT OFFICIAL (*Nervous.*): Yes, Lord... General. (*Reading.*) The nation is in crisis. Some, today, narrowly escaped... Ehm! We...we'll will come to that, General. (*Coughs.*) Our foreign trading partners missing...kidnapped. Pipeline's on fire. The villagers demanding more, and more ransom everyday. Now they want to be paid in dollars and pound sterling.
GENERAL: Nonsense!
GOVERNMENT OFFICIAL: Yes, Lord . Hear... hear it, now. From the horse's mouth.
GENERAL (*Yells.*) Yes, Police. Report?
POLICE (*Military salute but frightened.*) Got them...two prisoners.
GENERAL: Great! Continue.
OJI/POLICE (*Saluting.*): Yeaa-saaarp! Dangerous criminals. Old women Caught them. Prisoners. Yes. (*Takes chains out of his pocket.*) With these. Chained them. Yes. We chained them...locked them up.
GENERAL: Where?
OJI/POLICE: Maximum security saar.
GENERAL: So no problem. (*Orders the other Police Officer.*) Go immediately. Bring the prisoners here. Now!
OJI/POLICE (*Salutes, steps forward, stops.*) Saar...Oga.
GENERAL: Why stand there grinning like a goat-head on fire? I say go!
OJI/POLICE (*Frightened.*): But saar...oga. Not there. The prisoners dis...dis...nation...
GENERAL: The nation, what? (*Silence.*) Yes, I'm waiting. Tell me. What's happened to the nation?

OJI/POLICE: Dis...disappeared.
GENERAL: The Nation? Disappeared? Are you out of your mind?
OJI/POLICE (*Trembling.*): No...mind...gone... I mean the nation...
GENERAL: Precisely! (*Tense silence, then impatiently.*) Say...what's wrong with the nation?
OJI/POLICE (*Tries to steady himself.*): Criminals... Oga, criminals. Gone!
GENERAL: What? You let them escape?
OJI/POLICE: No saar. Dis...appear. Disappeared.
GENERA: How? What do you mean?
OJI/FIRST POLICE: Two old women...
SECOND POLICE: Witches.
GENERAL: You mean my Government now pays the police to arrest witches?
FIRST POLICE: Oh no...(*Saluting.*) Yes saar!
SECOND POLICE (*Pushing the other aside.*): No saar! He means...
FIRST POLICE (*Confronting his partner.*): Witch-hunting! Yes, that's what you're doing.
SECOND: Won't you let me finish?
FIRST POLICE: No, I won't. (*Saluting.*) Hear, saar. Don't mind him. He's ...he's lost. Crazy, my General. I'll tell you nothing...nothing but the truth.
GENERAL: Still waiting.
FIRST POLICE: As I was saying before he rudely interrupted. We got, chained the prisoners. Shameless old women who instead of staying quietly... in their homes...
SECOND: Graves!
GENERAL: Now shut up! And let him speak!
SECOND (*Saluting.*) Yes saaap!
GENERAL: With so many bas... idiots...What a country? (*He freezes, while the other chuckles, resumes his report.*)
FIRST POLICE: Chained. Chained them. Yes saar. My evidence? I have these chains to prove it, saar. (*Brandishing the chains.*) Here! But then the enemies are powerful...so powerful. Once we locked them up, they turned into dogs, you know, like those Security Dogs? (*The General is stunned and simply gives him a glare.*) Well, in the cell, the dogs started barking, barking, crying and wailing...even like human beings. God...General. Ah! In all my years, I've never seen or heard dogs bark like that. Those horrifying noises. Sounds that rip your heart open! Ah! So thinking the chains were too tight, we tried to untie... I mean loosen the chains a bit. Before we knew it, the gods...I mean, *dogs* were gone. How? Where? When? We don't know. Just

the chains. These chains. All we have left. So, what else could we do, my General.
GENERAL: Shoot! Shoot the blasted dogs. Criminals! That's what you're paid to do as police officers! Kill. Kill. Understand?
POLICEMEN (*Saluting.*): Yes, saar.
GENERAL: So repeat. What did I say?
POLICE (*Aims an imaginary gun.*) : Shoot! Shoot them!
GENERAL: On sight. Any time! Any place! At least, if you shoot them... dogs...That's all they are...
GOVERNMENT OFFICIAL: Except these International Civil...
GENERAL (*Screams.*): Nonsense!
GOVERNMENT OFFICIAL: Their rights!
GENERAL: Lies!
GOVERNMENT OFFICIAL: Rights saar...Their rights...
GENERAL: Bull sh...You heard him. He said they're dogs...turned gods...I mean...how can the state be prosecuted for killing dogs? Mere dogs, ehn!
CHIEF: Your Excellency, I understand. But we have to remember that...that this an elected government... by...for...the people... and all that. You know?
GENERAL: I don't...know a thing. And don't want to know.
CHIEF: As democrats...
GENERAL (*Incensed.*) Rats! That's all! (*Pause, threatening the Chief.*) Now, depart! You out of my sight! (*Chief, frightened, runs out. The General begins to pace up and down and is not addressing anyone in particular.*)
GENERAL: And the budget...our budget? How are we going to manage? With all the salary increase already announced? (*Firmly.*) Officials, note this.
(*They salute, write.*) No salary will be paid from now on until those people come to their senses! No salary will be paid. Yes! They'll suffer...suffer for this. Today, with immediate effect, I declare a state of emergency. Dawn to dusk curfew. Understand?
POLICEMEN (*Saluting.*): Yes saarp!
GENERAL: Go. Mobilize all Division One Brigade.
POLICEMEN: Yesaaarp! Sack the entire village. Shoot at sight!
POLICE: What?
GENERAL: I say shoot...shoot... anyone...anything... Living or dead. Shoot! Shoot at sight. Anybody. Nobody must be spared.
POLICE: Saar. Already, the whole nation... I mean village is under arrest. Old,

young...everybody. But the girls...Only those girls! And those old
˜women? Their ring leaders...But we'll get them.
GENERAL (*Shouting.*): All! Put all of them in custody!
POLICE: Your wish is my command! (*They salute, then march out.*)
GOVERNMENT OFFICIAL: Your Excellency. We must be cautious. The world... the world is watching...
GENERAL: Damn the whole blasted world! I rule...command...
GOVERNMENT OFFICIAL: Hooligan...Your Excellency! Just hooligans. Only a few... idiots... That's the problem.
GENERAL: Nonsense! Only a handful of terrorists and they're causing us all these damages? And now they're kidnapping our strange...I mean foreign business partners! And you know what that means to the image of this country. Shame. Shame! And more shame! (*Pensive.*) And our legacy? Hasn't the nation suffered enough already? (*Silence.*) Who next? Who knows? (*Pause.*) Can't you see? All this embarrassment? International disgrace? And we're only just trying to clean up our messy image before the whole world? Now these idiots—the so called activists are going to cry out about Human Rights abuses? Huh? Nonsense! They better know this. Their rights end where mine begin. Can't they see? Look who's abusing whom now? I'm ready. It's tit for tat. Go! Sack the entire village. Or better still, arrest all the criminals!
GOVERNMENT OFFICIAL: A great idea, your Excellency. That's much better.
GENERAL: So go now and arrest them.
POLICE: Who precisely?
GENERAL: Are you deaf? I said any one found in that village.
GOVERNMENT OFFICIAL: But your Excellency, remember we're being watched. The Press...The whole world...
GENERAL: Then blind-fold them.
GOVERNMENT OFFICIAL: The world?
GENERAL: Stop asking questions! This is our country!
GOVERNMENT OFFICIAL: Our democracy.
GENERAL: Damn demo-crazy! Slows down ...cripples everything! (*He sighs, paces, then stops. His mood changes.*) Ok. Their voice. Yes...their voice...We must show the world that people cannot take the law into their hands. Yes, we'll show our trading partners that we, too, are a nation of law and order. Criminals must not be allowed to go unpunished.
GOVERNMENT OFFICIAL: But their rights too...
GENERAL: I suppose... (*Sighs heavily.*) Ok. Lock up all the criminals.

(*Hitting the ground with his walking-stick.*) They will be tried. Everyone!
POLICE: The ringleaders are still at large.
GENERAL(*Ignoring him.*): Bloody activists making mincemeat of the state... administration...Saboteurs! All of them. Maybe they're even being paid by my past... I mean the last administration to ruin me. Ha! (*Screaming.*) Go find them! Find them! Bring them to me...On their knees. And that's *my* order! Or be stripped of your rank!
POLICE: When, saar?
GENERAL: Tomorrow.
POLICE: Yes, Lord... Excellency. Your will...be done. (*He salutes, marches out. War drums, and frenzied music/dance continues throbbing in the near distance. Lights snap.*)

# MOVEMENT TWELVE

(*As the people organize in the dark, more explosive sounds can be heard. Voices of protesting women and the youths can be heard. They're now ready to attack and they have ATLANTIC's gun. The Guard, and the fugitive or jailed women, too, have joined them. Thereafter, ATLANTIC enters, groping for the light that's now been cut off. Loud drumbeats and explosive sounds take over.*)

ATLANTIC: Say. What have they done this time? Who? Who took...took the light? (*Shouts.*): Guard! (*Silence.*) Security? Lights! (*Silence.*) Lights! (*Silence.*) Security, where are you? What's going on? (*Silence.* )
GOVERNMENT OFFICIAL (*Entering.*): What's *not* going on?
ATLANTIC: (*Startled.*): My God! You scared me!
GOVERNMENT OFFICIAL (*Agitated.*): I'm sorry. Crisis. Crisis. Listen my friend. (*War Drums break loose.*)
ATLANTIC (*Frightened.*): They're already here?
GOVERNMENT: No. They're marching.
ATLANTIC (*Alarmed.*): Where?
GOVERNMENT: On the streets.
ATLANTIC: They're coming? (*Sighs.*) I'm finished. Hold me. (*They support each other.*)
GOVERNMENT OFFICIAL: You're not alone.
(*Chanting and Drumming intensifies.*)
ATLANTIC (*Frantic.*) Finished. We're finished. (*Pause.*) What are they saying? What do they want?
GOVERNMENT: They say they too can do oil bunkering. They've set the Zone A oil pipeline on fire.
ATLANTIC (*Alarmed.*): What? The new plant?
GOVERNMENT OFFICIAL: Yes. (*Rising tension. Sounds of the protesters. ATLANTIC searches frantically for his gun. But he can't find it. Meanwhile, the protesting women led by OSHUN, OBIDA and KOKO approach with the guns .*)
ATLANTIC: Oh my God! My gun! That guard. The bloody thief must have stolen it. I'm gone! Gone! (*He's still searching for his weapon. Meanwhile, the explosive sounds continue, followed with loud drumbeats.*)
CHIEF (*Running.*): What are you going to do?
GOVERNMENT OFFICIAL: You can see there's no time to waste. The General has sent me here to summon you all.

ATLANTIC: And we have to go?
CHIEF: Do we have a choice?
ATLANTIC: I guess not.
GOVERNMENT OFFICIAL: No. (*Silence. They stare at each other.*)
GOVERNMENT OFFICIAL: Gentlemen, it's time for us to go. (*Exit Chief and Government Official. Some of the activists ambush and arrest them. While others, led by OSHUN and OBIDA invade the premises, and bind ATLANTIC's hands and feet, together, even as he struggles to be free.*)
ATLANTIC: You? You too? But I've been kind to you. Giving you my money?
OSHUN: Stolen from our land.
ATLANTIC: I see. You will regret this.
OSHUN: Re-what? Ha! Ha! Ha! Look at me now, ATLANTIC. Where? Where is your power? (*Displaying her chest.*) Shoot! Shoot! Shoot Lord Director!
ATLANTIC (*Spitefully.*): I will get you.
OSHUN: What? So he still has a mouth? Now get it. First! (*She slaps him. ATLANTIC swoons, bleeds.*)
OBIDA: No sister. No blood.
OSHUN: Yes. We must avoid violence.
OBIDA: Their game. Their style.
NIGER: Yes, children. We must not leave our dance to dance somebody else's dance. (*They start leading him away. OSHUN is soothing ATLANTIC, wiping away the blood.*)
OBIDA: Sorry about that, Mr. ATLANTIC Wilbros. Just one of those things...with young people. Can anyone stop youthful exuberance?
BENUE: Pay back time! What you people have done to us...to this land? (*Deep sigh.*)
ATLANTIC: Not me. I've done nothing.
OBIDA: Precisely! You've done nothing. Nothing good for this land.
KOKO: Except to take and take and take!
ATLANTIC: Look here. I did my part. I'm only here to represent an interest, you know. I'm not part of the system. Your government...
OBIDA: Your partners in crime.
OSHUN: You work with them. You eat with them.
OBIDA: Then get ready to die with them! (*Jumps to fight him.*)
NIGER (*Restraining her.*) OBIDA. Stop!
OBIDA (*Enraged.*) No, mother! Not now! You see? You know what they did to me?
BENUE: To us. We know. But calm. We'll see the light.

NIGER: At the end of the tunnel.
OSHUN (*Rather coy, takes up ATLANTIC's chin.*): Now, look into my face. Tell me. Tell us. How do you feel now?
ATLANTIC: Betrayed. Abandoned.
OBIDA: Like us? (*Silence.*)
NIGER: Then you're not alone, man.
BENUE: Makes us one. United.
OBIDA So welcome to the Club!
OSHUN: *Our* Club!
CHORUS: Of sufferers! Welcome, man!
OSHUN (*Like a reporter.*): And tell me, what is it that you want very much now?
ATLANTIC: Freedom. I want my freedom.
OBIDA: For how much? How much are you willing to pay?
ATLANTIC: Pay for what? I owe you nothing!
OBIDA: Ha! Ha! Ha! You don't?
ATLANTIC (*Sternly.*): Yes.
OBIDA: You'll soon find out.
ATLANTIC: Abuse my rights? Ah! You people. You better...Better set me free.
OBIDA: Just like that? Your freedom, *free*?
KOKO: When you people make us pay...
GUARD/YOUTH: For everything....
OSHUN: Even for the polluted air you make us breathe in this land.
OBIDA: Now it's time. Pay!
ATLANTIC: So what do you want? How much?
OBIDA: Three Billion.
ATLANTIC (*Stunned.*): What?
OSHUN: The price.
ATLANTIC: Ransom.
OSHUN: Wrong! Freedom costs.
ATLANTIC: Yours...
OSHUN: Ours!
ATLANTIC: You're much too demanding.
OSHUN: Really? Your friends know.
OBIDA: Ask them. They're waiting.
ATLANTIC (*Pressing the alarm button.*): Ah! They're here! Tell the Chief and the Government Official. Get them. Please get them.
OSHUN: For you? Or for us?
ATLANTIC (*Shocked.*) I...I... thought...for me. Where are they?
OBIDA: Waiting. (*Calls.*) KOKO! Where is she?
OSHUN: She's already there to take her place.

OBIDA: Great girl!
ATLANTIC: Please, the Chief. Where's he?
OSHUN: In her hands.
ATLANTIC: Whose?
OSHUN: My sister's. KOKO. You know her?
ATLANTIC (*Vehemently.*): I don't! What is there to know?
OBIDA: The Chief does. You'll know when the time comes.
ATLANTIC: When is that?
GUARD/YOUTH: When you pay.
ATLANTIC: Your ransom. How much?
OBIDA: We said *Three Billion.* Now!
OSHUN: No sister. It's not our way.
OBIDA: And our ransom? (*KOKO erects a banner from where they read aloud.*)
OSHUN: Food!
KOKO: Good roads! Not potholes!
BENUE: Clean water for cooking and drinking!
OBIDA: Clean air! Clean environment.
OSHUN: Yes. Unpolluted.
OBIDA: And Electricity?
OSHUN: So tell your people that unless they pay, you'll remain our guest.
OBIDA: For life! Ha! Ha! Ha!
  (*The women join her laughter. They start pulling him away.*)
KOKO: Ha, man. Know that you don't just take and take.
BENUE: Yes. You Give, and Take.
CHORUS: That's what life's all about!
KOKO: So now it's time to give...
CHORUS (*Singing and dancing.*): Give back! Give back!
OSHUN: That's how to live.
CHORUS: In freedom! For Freedom! Freedom!
OSHUN (*To NIGER & BENUE.*): Thank you mothers. Go. Leave the rest to us.
OBIDA: Yes, mothers. It's up to us now.
NIGER: & BENUE: We'll still take care.
OSHUN: But go. You know they're looking for you. Go now.
OBIDA: Mothers, remember your place. Stay in place.
NIGER & BENUE (*Departing.*): Yes, children. Take care. (*They're still chanting and dancing when the government forces swoop down and arrest OSHUN, OBIDA and the Guard, OSHUN's lover as the Bandit Boy.) The others escape. Blackout.*)

# EPILOGUE: A NATION IN CUSTODY

(*Sunrise. Siren sounds mixed with military music. Tension. Barricades as stage opens, revealing the lounge at the Oil Club, now turned Supreme Court, awaiting the trial of the prisoners. The screen shows flashes of a very rowdy mob, struggling to get through the barricades but can't. For a while, their charged voices fill the air:*
"Free! Free! Free our women! Free!
Free free the mothers! Free! Free!
The Sisters! Free! Free! Say Freeeeeeedooooom!"
ETHIOPE *is already on stage, trying out robes, ties and other paraphernalia in preparation for his new role as the Trial Justice. The Lounge table has been raised and draped with white cloth. Unknown to them all, the escaped prisoners,* NIGER *and* BENUE *have bribed the police officer to take the jailed youths,* OBIDA *and* OSHUN *out of the cell. Now, as they await the trial of their people, all the escapees have reorganized and positioned themselves under the draped lounge table, ready to strike. Then suddenly, the* GENERAL/ATLANTIC *walks in with a swagger and a stick.*)

ETHIOPE/JUSTICE (*Startled.*): My God....Your Excellency! Aaaah!
GENERAL (*Smiling.*): Justice Alpha. I didn't mean to scare you, of all people.
ETHIOPE/JUSTICE (*Uneasy.*): Ehnm... Ok. Your...Ex...Just that I wasn't expecting you here.
GENERAL: I rule this country, you know. Any problem?
ETHIOPE/JUSTICE: Ah yes! No. Ehnmm....just this mob.
GENERAL: I know.
GENERAL: A nuisance. A great nuisance!
JUSTICE: Like an itch in the eye?
GENERAL: Delicate. Quite delicate, I know. (*Pause.*) But atimes, one may have to break an eyeball that itches. Not so?
JUSTICE: Not, normally.
GENERAL (*Impatiently.*): In military circumstances, we do. We have to.
JUSTICE (*Smiling.*): Except this is a...
GENERAL (*Defensively.*): Democratic government...as they say. (*Drawing near, confiding in the Justice.*)
Look my friend. I know how you feel...Justice, democracy fairness and all that.
JUSTICE: Not to talk of the fact that the whole world is watching us now. (*The Justice is now fully robed.*)

GENERAL: Yes. To see us fail. But we won't. With your co-operation, we won't.
JUSTICE: Promise.
GENERAL: All we need is to give the world out there an appearance of justice. I mean fairness.
JUSTICE: Under the constitution, the suspects...
GENERAL (*Correcting.*): Criminals!
JUSTICE: Oh, well. Deemed innocent until...
GENERAL: Proven guilty. I hear.
JUSTICE: The prisoners deserve a fair trial.
GENERAL: Granted. (*Brief pause, then raised stern voice.*) Criminals! That's what they are. (*Bitterly.*) These bastards want to ruin me? My regime? Perhaps they're even paid by my opponents and past administration to incite...subvert the good progress we're making in this administration? (*As they speak, the tension outside intensifies.*)
JUSTICE: And the people's rights? Look General. The people's right of speech is part of that progress.
GENERAL: Oh no! Nobody says the people have no rights. But rights must be measured...I mean...moderated. No we can't deny that. But what this administration will not tolerate is people defending, I mean taking the law into their hands in the name of rights.
JUSTICE: Self-protection. Remember.
GENERAL (*Passionately.*): Look, Justice. All that I understand. But remember too that nobody is above the law.
JUSTICE (*Smiling*): Precisely! That's why we must put that into practice. Our nation is already too stigmatized before the people, before the international community. Human rights, abuses, massive imprisonment without trial. Now...
GENERAL (*Impatiently.*): All that must be reversed. And you alone hold the key to all that.
JUSTICE: How? As a Judge, my job is to try ...
GENERAL (*Closely, passionately.*): The criminals! Saboteurs! Can't you see? I have reports. They're paid. Paid to ruin you...and me, I have it here. (*He pulls out a list from his pocket.*). Yes we are a nation on trial. This must stop. The image of the nation has been beaten, battered and fried in the court of public opinion. Now we must rescue, and heal it. You and me. Promise? (*He waits for it to sink in as the Justice stands, weighing his words*). Is it not obvious? Where? Where has it ever happened that illiterate rural women...women and mere girls rise up in arms against elected and established government? Women, mili-

tarized? Haba, Judge! Where have you ever heard that? Ehn? Look, if they had revolted during the last military democracy...I mean... military dictatorship, I could...

JUSTICE: Understand...

GENERAL: But trust me. The problem of women... And rights? Cancerous growth in the belly of the land. And illiterate women for that matter? How? This has never happened before. I tell you, these women are not acting alone. They're paid rebels. Seditionists... As they say, the dancer on the road has a drummer in a nearby bush.

JUSTICE: True General. But their rights...

GENERAL (*Irritated.*): Lies! (*Pause.*) What rights?

JUSTICE: Women's...

GENERAL: Oh, come on! Don't be fooled by those Feminist nonsense. Jargons! Feminists? (*Spits.*) Rabble rousers! Worst of women. Failed, frustrated women. All of them. Ugly. Old maids. Watch. Watch them. Nowadays when women fail to find husbands, or fail in their marriages, they turn feminists. Even les...bians! (Spits) Abominable! With that, they start spitting fire and hatred against men. And you know, they demonize what they lose, can't reach or get. That's what the so-called feminists do, if you asked me.

JUSTICE (*Stunned.*): Interesting. A most interesting post modern...post patriarchal ideology. The bottom line is their rights. (*Pause.*) They're masking mourning then?

GENERAL: All must wait. All rights must come after me... I mean my administration. (*Pleads.*) Look, you are a JUSTICE. Execute the women.

JUSTICE: The Law, you mean?

GENERAL: Yes. Execute all. Everything. Everyone.

JUDGE; Without trial?

GENERAL: Tried. Life sentence? Sure I'm game. (*Passionately.*) Here. Name your terms. In addition I will name you to the Supreme Court. (*He waits for his reaction.*) Promise? You are after all, Justice Omega...The very best in this land.

JUSTICE (*Loud laughter.*): And you the Alpha!

GENERAL: We stay united. (*Serenading.*) To keep Hungeria one?

JUSTICE: Is a task that must be done!

GENERAL & JUSTICE: All hail Hungeria! (*They both laugh, exchange clapping salute and embrace. Music swells in the background as the General/ATLANTIC departs. Immediately the lounge table jerks forward. The women appear in their white shroud, seize the Trial Justice him, disrobe him and quickly bind him, hands and feet. They put ordi-*

nary clothes on him, then push him behind. NIGER now helps OBIDA into the gown of the Trial Judge while BENUE assists KOKO into the legal outfit of the Defense Lawyer. As the girls begin to quickly adjust to their new roles as Trial Judge and Defense Lawyer, the older women vanish into the crowded community of prisoners. Now the martial sounds. The trial is about to begin as the legal actors respectively take their place at the appropriate moment: OJI as the state Prosecutor, ETHIOPE as the traditional Chief, OSHUN, NIGER, BENUE and KAINJI/Bandit Boy as the lead-prisoners. The police takes position at the court entrance. Outside, the screen shows the screaming hysterical mob as they march into the courthouse with their victory song: "Onye Akpana nwagu aka nodu! M'Odindu. M'Onwu lanwu! Onye akpana nwagu aka nodu!." Lights change as the transformed OBIDA/Trial Judge, now mounts the legal bench to face the audience who will serve as the jury for this trial. Then the Police calls out: "All rise!". They obey. "The court is now in session. Let the trial begin," the judge announces. ETHIOPE/Chief is led to a seat. KOKO/Defense Lawyer now serves him the papers.)

OBIDAJUSTICE (To the Police.): Bring the prisoners in. (First, the chained NIGER, BENUE and OSHUN are led in with the Bandit Boy.) The people's Court wishes to declare open the Trial Number 111 of the new Millennium. (Reading.) Today, this court will begin with the case of the People against the State.

OJI/PROSECUTOR: Your honor. Point of correction. It's the 'State of Hungeria against the People'.

OBIDA/JUSTICE: Do I take it that I'm the trial Judge here?

OJI/PROSECUTOR: Yes, Your Honor.

OBIDA/JUSTICE: And the people are being tried before me?

OJI/PROSECUTOR: Yes. But your honor...

OBIDA/JUSTICE (Sternly.): I will not be interrupted. And if you insist, you will be charged with "Contempt of this Court," Counsel, understand?

OJI/PROSECUTOR: I do. (With this development, the mob screams: "All Hail Justice! All Hail Freedom!")

OBIDA/JUSTICE (Firmly.): Order! This is a court of law, not a marketplace! (Immediate silence.). Will the plaintiffs present their case?

OBIDA/JUSTICE: There are numerous charges and counter-charges. The People Vs the State. (The Prosecutor rises and struts around the space, then takes a stand. For a moment before he speaks, one by one, he looks sternly at the prisoners, chained and arraigned before the court. Meanwhile, KOKO as Defense Lawyer sits quietly. The Prosecutor

105

takes a roll-call of the prisoners, who in turn answer 'present'. )
OJI/PROSECUTOR (*Calling out names with each one answering 'present!'*): OSHUN! NIGER! BENUE! KAINJI! (*To the Judge.*) Apart from the fugitive suspects...
OBIDA/JUSTICE: You have their names?
OJI/PROSECUTOR: Yes your honor. Here. (*Reads.*) The State wishes the court to note that some more dangerous criminals are still at large, missing.
OBIDA/JUSTICE (*Writing.*): You know them?
OJI/PROSECUTOR: Women. Two of them, old hags, I should say, are here. (*Throws spiteful looks at NIGER and BENUE.*)
OBIDA/JUSTICE (*Writing.*): Their names?
OJI/PROSECUTOR: NIGER, and BENUE.
OBIDA/JUSTICE: Will the suspects NIGER and BENUE stand? (*The prisoners try to stand. But the chains pull them down and they fall. Then rise up painfully again.*)
OBIDA/JUSTICE (*Writing.*): I see. (*Pause.*) You may sit. Counsel, proceed.
OJI/PROSECUTOR: Apart of those two who are still at large, your honor, I present to you the felons. OSHUN and KAINJI, popularly known as the Bandit Boy. These vandals have been tyrannizing the state, with its foreign partners for sometime now. These criminals have been threatening the peace of the land. Breaking down law and order. Engaging in arson. Kidnapping of innocent law-abiding citizens and foreigners as they derive pleasure in burning down public property. In short, Your Honor, these criminals have been charged with a million counts of felonies for their nefarious, irresponsible acts to bring down this proud nation to becoming a laughing stock before the global community.
KOKO/DEFENSE LAWYER (*Rising.*): Objection, your honor. The plaintiff is misleading the court and making provocative false, malicious presumptive charges to prejudice the court against my clients.
OBIDA/JUSTICE: Objection sustained. Counsel, you may proceed.
OJI/PROSECUTOR: Your Honor, May I?
OBIDA JUSTICE: No. Counsel. Be advised to save our time and proceed with your argument.
OJI/PROSECUTOR: Hnm.. Well... I now present to this court the abundant evidence before us. (*He shows and circulates pictures of the state casualties*) As the evidence shows and proves beyond any reasonable doubt, the State hereby charges and insists that these felons be convicted and found guilty on the following counts: Arson, Kidnapping, Assault, Burglary, and Sabotage against national progress.

Assembled before you are the plagues afflicting this great nation. And like any pestilence, Your Honor, the state is duty-bound to wipe them out before they contaminate and ruin the soul and body of the land. Therefore, as stipulated in the constitution, under Section 7, Subsection 1998 and as evidenced in the case of Sonny General Against the People, June 8, 1998, we pray the court that these criminals be executed summarily...

KOKO/DEFENSE LAWYER: Objection! My learned colleague has chosen to incite, mislead and manipulate the opinion of this court against my poor clients.

OBIDA/JUSTICE: Objection sustained. Proceed, Counsel.

OJI/PROSECUTOR: Hmn...With mounting evidence proved beyond reasonable doubt, these felons deserve Capital Punishment. Or at least, to be sentenced to life imprisonment for their atrocious acts against the state, and as a means of healing and restoring the faith and wounded spirit of our land. On these grounds, Your Honor, the prosecution will rest its case.

OBIDA/JUSTICE *(To the prisoners.)*: You have heard the grave charges against you. Do you plead guilty or not guilty?

PRISONERS *(Chorus.)*: **Not Guilty**!

OBIDA/JUSTICE *(Writing.):* The court notes that all the suspects have pleaded *Not Guilty*. Now, Counsel, do you have any witness to testify to your charges?

PROSECUTOR: Oh, yes, your honor. Many. My witnesses are waiting.

OBIDA/JUSTICE: They can wait. *(To the Defense Lawyer.)* Does the Defense team have any information for this court at the moment?

KOKO/DEFENSE LAWYER: No, Your Honor. We can wait. My clients have been waiting. For life. Doing time. But their own time shall come. So we decline to speak at this moment.

OBIDA/JUSTICE: Then proceed, Counsel.

OJI/PROSECUTOR: Thank you, Your Honor. *(He motions to the police to produce their first witness. The police leaves and quickly returns with the tired and frazzled looking ATLANTIC. As soon as he's produced, voices of protest become amplified. The Judge calls for order. The protests die down, and ATLANTIC is made to swear and mount the witness box to give evidence.)*

OJI/PROSECUTOR: Please tell your full name to this court.

ATLANTIC: My name is ATLANTIC White Western.

OJI/PROSECUTOR: Your address?

ATLANTIC: Crude oil... I mean Number One, On-Shore Oil Club Villa, the

GRA Oil Club, Hungeria Federation.
OJI/PROSECUTOR: What is your professional title and what do you do for a living?
ATLANTIC: I am Director of the International Crude Guild in Hungeria. My business is Drilling, Selling, Buying and Marketing oil to the global community.
OJI/PROSECUTOR: What type of oil?
ATLANTIC: The Hungerian Crude Sweet.
OJI/PROSECUTOR: In what location?
ATLANTIC: In-land and off-shore as approved and contracted with the government of the land.
OJI/PROSECUTOR: Mr. ATLANTIC, please tell this court what you have experienced for some time now in conducting your rightful business?
ATLANTIC: In recent months, especially, I have been molested, harassed, robbed, brutalized. My associates have been kidnapped by these vandals. Personal unprecedented losses.
OJI/PROSECUTOR: Please Director, give this court an estimate of your loss?
ATLANTIC: Billions. This month alone, we have lost more than 10 million dollars.
OJI/PROSECUTOR: And?
ATLANTIC: And lives. My colleagues...members of the cartel...
OJI/PROSECUTOR: Local or foreign?
ATLANTIC: All foreign. Foreigners with right to decent life and property in this...this... lawless... (*Breaking down Prosecutor helps him to his seat.*)
OJI/PROSECUTOR (*To the Court.*): That was...is Mr. ATLANTIC. As you can see, my client has been traumatized, brutalized and victimized by these criminals, with neither respect for any life nor property. Your Honor, how can anyone with such despicable criminal records be allowed to go free and unpunished? (*Pause.*) Your Honor, at this moment, we'd like to call to the witness box the one called KAINJI, a lead member of the criminal gang. He's popularly called, The Bandit Boy.
(*OSHUN's lover takes his place on the witness stand.*)
OJI/PROSECUTOR: What is your name?
BANDIT BOY: Whatever you think or say I am.
OJI/ PROSECUTOR: What? Answer my question. (*Sternly.*) What is your name?
BANDIT BOY: I already said it. (*Prosecutor pulls down his glasses below his nose, gives the boy a hard look and continues.*)
OJI/PROSECUTOR: What do you do for a living?
BANDIT BOY: Ha! What do I do for a living?

OJI/PROSECUTOR: Yes.
BANDIT BOY: Am I living? Ha! Ha! Ha!
OJI/PROSECUTOR: Well, tell the court.
BANDIT BOY: And you think I'm *living*?
OJI/PROSECUTOR: Now stop evading the question and...
BANDIT BOY: Ok. I'll show you. (*In a swift motion, he gives the lawyer a push, knocks him down to the floor. Quickly, he impounds the man's briefcase and tries to escape as the Judge screams "Catch him! Catch!" The police is at hand to get him.*)
OBIDA/JUSTICE: Nobody, not even the prosecutor is allowed to take the law into his hands. Therefore, the witness is hereby charged with...
BANDIT BOY (*Exploding.*): What? Again? It's unfair. You all were here. He asked me to tell the court what I do for a living. And that's what I did. Show him! All I did was his bidding. Obeyed. Showed you just that. What I do for a living. So what else have I done wrong? Where again have I gone wrong? Is there no place, nothing that a poor boy can do right in this land without justice?
OJI/PROSECUTOR: My Lord, and fellow citizens. You're all witnesses. You've seen it with your own eyes. A hostile witness, with no respect for the rule of law. He is a most dangerous convict. I hereby urge the court to charge him with Contempt of Court. And more so, sentence him to the Firing Squad for all his brutal muder of innocent citizens. Nothing more needs be said. The state shall rest its case for now.
OBIDA/JUSTICE: The court has taken note of your plaintiffs' request. And the defendant's position too. This court will rule on this case before proceeding to the others. Until he spoke, the state assumed that everyone had an answer to such a simple question as : "What do you do for a living". Well, granted the defendant was too dramatic in response to the question. But then, there is some truth in what he did. To actually *show* what he did for a *living*. And as implied, the defendant contests the assumption that he is living. So what do we mean by living? The defendant has opened up that point of controversy for us to ponder. Are we all living? If so, how? Let me leave it at that. I hereby withdraw my earlier ruling on the defendant's conduct. Let the jury think about it, rule on that on your own. (*Pause.*) Next? (*Prosecutor goes to sit down. KOKO as Defense Lawyer, now rises to take the stand. As soon as she rises, the prisoners chant once again but the Trial Judge halts them.*)
KOKO/ DEFENSE (*Eloquent, dignified.*): Your Honor. Country men and women. Fellow citizens of the world. And thank you, my Learned

Friend. You have heard the fictional charges cooked up by my learned friend and the powerful in state to annihilate, exterminate a whole community as if they were pests. Now before you all, I present the people. These traumatized people who have been struggling with these powers that beat and keep them down to let them be free, let them have decent jobs. Food. Water. Electricity. Roads. Life. Just the bare minimum for survival. *(Spotlight on each prisoner as she points to them with one hand and holds up a can of insecticide on the other. Then KOKO, the Defense lawyer turns to the Jury.)* Just look...look at them. Do any of these look to you like mosquitoes?
VOICES: No!
KOKO/DEFENSE LAWYER: Do they look like bugs or pests to you?
VOICES: No!
KOKO/DEFENSE LAWYER: Do they look like animals to you?
OJI/PROSECUTOR: Not just animals but beasts. Beasts! *(Voices of protest rise again. The judge intervenes. Prosecutor is petrified, screams.)* Is this a trial...kangaroo court or...
OBIDA/JUSTICE *(Firmly.)*: Stop! The Prosecutor is hereby fined 1000 bonds for contempt of court. With apologies for questioning the integrity of this court. Now! *(Silence.)*
OJI/PROSECUTOR: Your Honor. Is this an inquest? Well...ehm...Sorry...*(Pays fine.)*
OBIDA/JUSTICE: Counsel, you may now proceed.
KOKO/DEFENSE LAWYER: I see. Now we'd like to request that the prosecutor's witness be brought back here. *(ATLANTIC is returned to the witness box. Defense lawyer offering the can of insecticide to the Prosecutor, then to ATLANTIC.)* Here. Take. Feel free. Spray as you have always to pollute the land, the environment. And wipe out anything and anyone in your way...outside your interest. *(Silence, as ATLANTIC gazes into space.)* Yes, spray on.
OJI/PROSECUTOR: Objection, your honor! We're being intimidated.
OBIDA/JUSTICE: Objection, overruled! Counsel may proceed.
KOKO/DEFENSE LAWYER: For nearly half a century, Your Honor, the living mothers, sons and daughters of the land have been trampled. Oppressed. Exploited. And dehumanized. You're all witnesses. Since the Sweet Crude was discovered in their land, everyone of them has had their own personal tragic experiences. They've been without jobs, farming and fishing resources...painful, hard experiences that progressively changed their lives for the worse. My fellow citizens, it is not for me to tell, for as they say, she who wears the shoe knows

where it pinches. My learned friend, reinforced by his prosecution witness has presented these poor women and youths as the nagging pestilence and diseases afflicting this land. Now before you all, they stand. Helpless. Poverty-stricken. Shackled. Mothers, sons and daughters of this land who have become prisoners of the state, foreign and private interests. Here they are. (*Calling.*) OSHUN! (*As they're called, each prisoner* answers "Here!".) NIGER! BENUE! KAINJI! (*Lawyer turns to the jury.*) As you can see, unlike the views of my Learned Friend—who labels them animals and who neither knows nor calls them by their names, each one of them is fully human. With blood. Feeling. Emotion. Pain. And what more? Everyone of them has a name, with meaning, which I don't wish to repeat or dwell on here. See them. They are all living human beings. With equal rights to live. Eat. Make love. Money. And babies. And families. Just as the rich, mighty and powerful interests that stifle them. Look. What separates them from you? The only difference continues to be their drying blood, Drilled. Sapped. Plundered. And sold by you, the powerful state and foreign interests to ensure your gains! With every sale, sapping or siphoning, the people get weaker and weaker and anemic, as you the rich and powerful suck them dry and get stronger and stronger. At the center of it all? Money! Profit! Power! That, in a nutshell is the basic difference! The root of the millennium disease in this land. I call it the MPP! Money. Profit. Power. The pandemic! That, my people is the triple valley separating our world of the poor from the rich. With MPP, our world is carved, sold and auctioned by the rich and powerful. And today, only two tribes or races exist in our world; the Tribe or Race of the Rich Vs the Poor! Our Market Culture has emerged. And in this culture, the rich are 'colorless'. Color-less! In this, the poor become imprisoned and sentenced to life by the rich (*Pause.*) Fellow citizens of the world. I am only an intermediary between the law and the people. I'm only an interpreter of the law. But the people are here. Now. I cannot speak for them. Let them speak. (*To the prisoners.*) Now it's time. Your time. Speak for yourselves! Speak. Who can Silence the drums? Delta Women, Speak! (*The prisoners voices rise in unison. They stand, holding each other to form a human chain and then raise a chant/dirge that tells their plight. But the judge soon stops them. NIGER stands, weighed down and weakened by her chained arms. On her clenched teeth, she carries the picture of her murdered son and husband, which she tries to wave up and down as she tries to speak with the wedge on her lips.*)

NIGER: Hnmm....Hnmmm... (*She's trembling, her voice muffled. Sensing her difficulties, the Judge urges her on.*)
OBIDA/JUSTICE: Speak, NIGER! It's your time. (*But still overwhelmed by her burden, the woman stumbles and mumbles something again.* )
KOKO/DEFENSE LAWYER: Your Honor. As you can see, my clients are weighed down, encumbered by the weight of evidence latched on to their lips. And before I proceed, I pray the court to untie my clients. Free them from the shackles. At least in the democratic world, suspects are presumed innocent until convicted. Not so?
OJI/PROSECUTOR: Objection! They're dangerous! They fled, escaped many times from the jail.
OBIDA/JUSTICE: Objection denied! The Defense is right. (*To the Police.*) Untie them. Release them from the chains. Counsel, proceed. (*The Prisoners are untied.*)
KOKO/DEFENSE LAWYER (*Gathering all the suspects' pictures.*): Your Honor. Here are the exhibits. The tormented faces here to speak for themselves. Do I have the permission of the court to show...present the exhibits?
OBIDA/JUSTICE: You may. (*Defense Lawyer starts circulating the pictures.*)
KOKO/DEFENSE LAWYER: Your Honor, shall I request that from now till the end, we reverse the proceedings into an Open Trial.
OBIDA/JUSTICE: What do you mean?
KOKO/DEFENSE LAWYER: In short, Your Honor. I propose this. Let the Defendants directly interrogate the prosecution...the prosecution witnesses.
OBIDA/JUSTICE: If you may.
OJI/PROSECUTOR: Objection!
OBIDA/JUSTICE: Denied! The defense can go on.
KOKO/DEFENSE LAWYER: Thank you, Your Honor. (*To the prisoners.*). It's time now. Speak.
NIGER (*Sighs heavily, then her lips break loose.*): My people, My name is NIGER. I am the leader of the market women. I used to be strong, beautiful. See me now. See what I have become because of what they have dome to me. To us. Abused. Mother raped. Daughter raped. And raped. Son slaughtered. Husband roasted. Alive. (*Sighs heavily.*) My body aches. My heart bleeds. But I'm not alone. Though we suffer together, each one of us here do have our own scars. Scars. Scars. Telling our own peculiar stories. (*Silence.*) Our stories are so long that if we all were to speak and tell the world all that we have been through, our narratives would never end. So now, we can only share

with you a bite. Just a small bite as evidence of what eats deep within us. (*Raised Voice.*) Mothers, sons and daughters of Oilland, do I speak your voice?
CHORUS of PRISONERS: Yes!
NIGER: Did you elect me your representative?
CHORUS OF PRISONERS: Yes!
NIGER: Should I speak our collective voices?
CHORUS OF PRISONERS: Yes!
NIGER (*She asks to lift the released photo.*): Look at those pictures again. My hero. My burden. That was my husband. The father of my children. This too was my son, bubbling with flesh and blood. Do they not look strong? Handsome? Respectable? (*Silence.*) But where are they now? (*Silence.*) Where! (*Silence.*) Can I ask the Whiteman, and the Chief, together with their friend, the mouthpiece of the state. Where? Where is my husband? And my son? Where? Where are the men? (*Silence.*) Oga, why do you remain silent? You took my son and husband. (*Passionately.*) Took them. My love. My life. You know what you did with them. Why? Why? Why do you kill innocent men, women and children? Why? (*To the prisoners.*) You are now free. Let the world hear your stories. Tell your stories. Who can silence the drums? Delta women speak! (*Immediately, their tongues break loose as each one speaks his or her pain, experience and condition. This is not scripted but improvised and enacted to reflect each person's uniqueness and creativity, even as they build into a chorus.*)
CHORUS OF PRISONERS" Why? Why? Why?
NIGER: Tell the world why?
CHORUS OF PRISONERS: Why? Why? Why?
NIGER: Speak, you rich and powerful men who ride on the painful back of others. Speak! You who drink and dine on the blood of others. What you did. Why you did....
CHORUS OF PRISONERS: Why? Why? Why?
(*No longer able to keep silent and take the trauma, ATLANTIC's lips break loose.*)
ATLANTIC: I didn't!
NIGER: So who did it?
ATLANTIC: Ask the state...Your representatives. I am not responsible. I paid. Paid dearly for all I got.
NIGER: When? To whom? How much?
ATLANTIC: It's not for me to say. However little, we paid either what we were told was due, or was the worth.

NIGER: And that is?
ATLANTIC: Nothing...Nothing I can say...
CHORUS: Tell! Tell us! Tell now. The world is waiting!
ATLANTIC: I paid not only to the middleman...Businessman, the government, but to the leaders. *Your* leaders...
CHORUS OF PRISONERS: Who?
ATLANTIC: Your leaders...(*Hesitates.*) The Government Official and the Chief, for example.
CHORUS OF PRISONERS: Ohooo! The Thief! We want them! We want justice! Bring the so-called leaders! Here! Here! Her! Let them speak!
OBIDA/JUSTICE: Now is the time. (*To the Defense Lawyer.*) Shall we have the Chief and his friend?
OJI/PROSECUTION: Objection! The Chief is our Prosecution witness.
OBIDA/JUSTICE: Overruled! Let justice take its course. (*To the Police.*) Bring the witness here. (*In anger, the prosecuting lawyer stages a dignified walkout. Quickly, the Chief and the Government Official go into the witness box. NIGER steps down from the witness box. Quite unexpectedly, OBIDA/Justice, steps out of her role and place to lead the interrogation of the witnesses.*)
OBIDA/JUSTICE: Will the Defense please allow this bench a few helpful questions.
KOKO DEFENSE LAWYER (*Stepping aside.*): You have the floor, Your Honor.
OBIDA/JUSTICE (*To ATLANTIC.*): White man, repeat your charges against these people.
ATLANTIC: I have no changes against them. All I said is that I paid them, each of them at different times for different things.
OBIDA/JUSTICE: Like what precisely?
ATLANTIC: The farmlands.
OBIDA/JUSTICE: Ahh! To *whom* did you pay?
ATLANTIC (*Stuttering.*): Your Honor must I...? Must I answer these people? They're...they're...
OBIDA JUSTICE: (*Smiling.*): Human beings! People with a voice to speak and ask questions for themselves. They too, have the permission of the court to speak. (*To the Defense Lawyer.*) Proceed with your questions.
CHIEF (*Aside, to The Government Official.*): These terrible women. Everywhere you are, you meet them coming. You meet them going.
ATLANTIC: For example, I paid the Chief for the farmlands.
OBIDA/JUSTICE (*Breaking into mock laughter.*): Chief *Thief*! Ha! Ha! Ha!

Chief. Did you hear that? (*Silence.*) What do you have to say for yourself? Now defend yourself.
CHIEF (*Vexed.*): I have done nothing to deserve...
OBIDA/JUSTICE: Any good or justice. But you took money from him. For what?
CHIEF: For services rendered.
OBIDA/JUSTICE: Ahaaah! Services! Paid services! To whom? For whom?
CHIEF: The people.
OBIDA/JUSTICE: Whose people?
CHIEF: *My* people.
OBIDA/JUSTICE (*Indicating herself.*): Including this one? (*Silence.*) Yes, Chief. Father of the people. Defender of the land. Do you remember the this face? (*OBIDA takes off her wig and other camouflage. She approaches the Chief. He is stunned, terrified.*)
CHIEF: O...BID...!!!! Ha-ha-ha! (*Silence. The Chief is horrified by the sight of the scarified woman before him.*)
OBIDA: Yes. OBIDA. The same one you sold.
CHIEF (*Gasping.*): What? Is this...what? What happened...what did they do to you?
OBIDA: No Uncle...Father. It's not others who did it to me. To us. But you.
CHIEF: Me?
OBIDA: Yes! You father! Burnt me. Raped me!
KOKO/DEFENSE LAWYER (*Stripping her own mask.*): Raped me too! (*The Chief recognizes her too, falls as he grips them both. OSHUN now joins them.*)
CHORUS OF WOMEN (*Chanting.*): Yes, let our daughters speak! Speak for us!
OBIDA, OSHUN & KOKO (*To ATLANTIC and the Government Official.*): And you too? Remember? See? See your bloody handiwork? (*The men are stupefied. The women and youths have risen into choral chants. The drum beats rise slowly. The Chief, Government Official and ATLANTIC are trembling.*)
CHIEF (*To ATLANTIC.*): But... but...I gave you...
GOVERNMENT OFFICIAL: Oh God! Oh God!
ATLANTIC: Save! Save me!
CHIEF (*Gasping.*): Forgive...daughters! Sisters, forgive! Never! Never again! I shouldn't... shouldn't have...My people! I failed...failed to defend...
GOVERNMENT OFFICIAL: If we had to do it all over?
ATLANTIC: It will never be the same.
GOVERNMENT OFFICIAL: Now we know.

CHIEF: Oh yes we know.
CHIEF (*Delirious, muttering.*): Forgive...Forgive...Forgive...
ATLANTIC: We need...need...talk. Let's talk...
GOVERNMENT OFFICIAL: Yes. We'll create jobs.
CHIEF: Pay you.
ATLANTIC: Compensation.
CHORUS OF THE PEOPLE: We must have our resource! Resource Control! Resource Control!
OSHUN: About time!
OBIDA: All we ask of you is just to live. Live with dignity in life. And that's what these women and youths have always wanted. But no. In your own way, you stand in their way. In my way. In everybody's way. Because you have the power and the money. Is it fair? Where did we go wrong?
CHORUS OF THE PEOPLE: Where? Where did we go wrong? What did we do wrong?
OSHUN: Is poverty a crime?
OBIDA: Is it?
CHORUS: Is it? Is poverty-poverty a crime!
OBIDA/OSHUN (*To their target.*): You tell us.
CHORUS: Tell us-tell us-tell us...Is poverty a crime?
OSHUN: Is it?
CHORUS: Is it? Is it? Is *it*?
OBIDA: And so she said it!
CHORUS: She said it-Said it-Then She Said it! (*Pause.*) Is it? (*With spotlights on them in this call-response chant, the rousing drumbeats empower the women and youths into a huge orchestra as they shift out of the stage and into the audience, to build into a communal dance-party until floodlights.*)

www.ingramcontent.com/pod-product-compliance
Lightning Source LLC
Chambersburg PA
CBHW061959220426
43662CB00011B/1739